Eyewitness
ANCIENT CIVILIZATIONS

Mycenaean
gold brooch

Ancient Phoenician
glass pendant

Large Moche
earring

Greek philosophers
Plato (left) and
Aristotle (right)

Ancient Egyptian
gaming table

Minoan jars from
Akrotiri, Greece

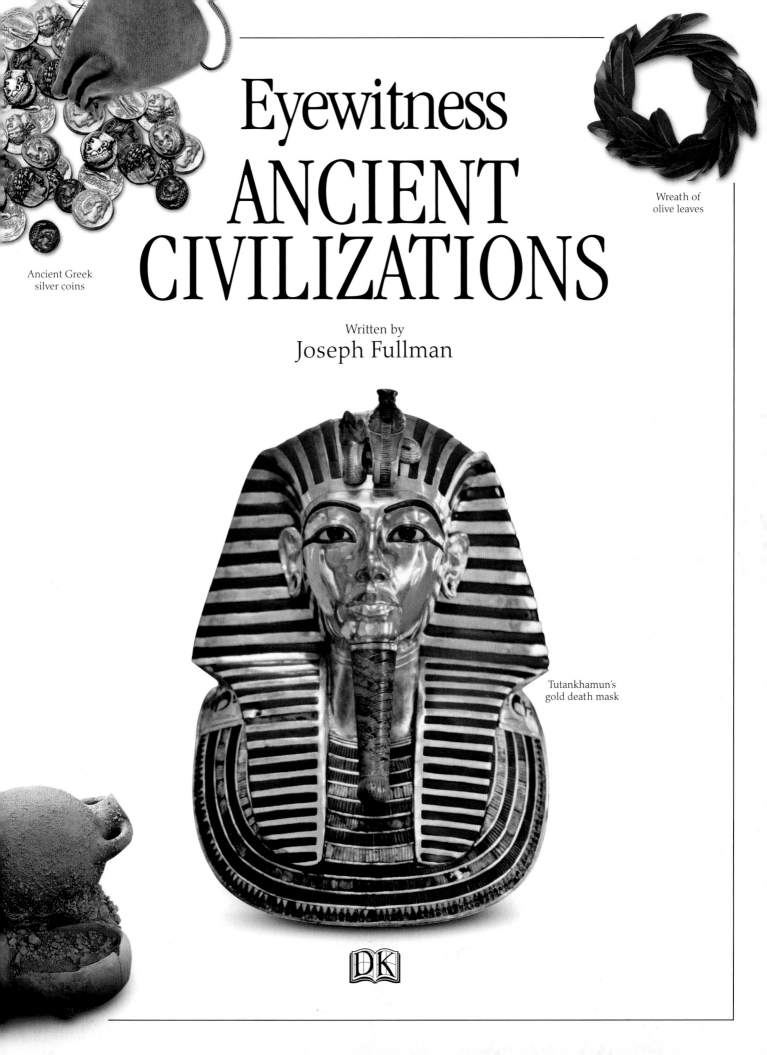

Ancient Greek
silver coins

Eyewitness
ANCIENT
CIVILIZATIONS

Wreath of
olive leaves

Written by
Joseph Fullman

Tutankhamun's
gold death mask

DK

Roman javelin (top) and
thrusting spear (bottom)

Roman *gladius*, a short sword

LONDON, NEW YORK,
MELBOURNE, MUNICH, AND DELHI

Consultant John Haywood

DK DELHI

Project editor Shatarupa Chaudhuri
Project art editor Nishesh Batnagar
Assistant editor Priyanka Kharbanda
Assistant art editor Honlung Zach Ragui
Senior art editor Govind Mittal
Senior DTP designer Tarun Sharma
DTP designer Neeraj Bhatia
DTP manager Sunil Sharma
Managing editor Alka Thakur
Managing art editor Romi Chakraborty
Production manager Pankaj Sharma
Picture researcher Sumedha Chopra

DK LONDON

Senior editors Caroline Stamps, Rob Houston
Senior art editor Rachael Grady
Publisher Andrew Macintyre
Pre-production producer Adam Stoneham
Production controller Charlotte Cade
Jacket designer Jessica Park

DK US

Project editor Margaret Parrish
Editorial director Nancy Ellwood

First American Edition, 2013
Published in the United States by DK Publishing
345 Hudson Street, New York, New York 10014

13 14 15 16 17 10 9 8 7 6 5 4 3 2 1

187508—July/13

A catalog record for this book is available
from the Library of Congress.

ISBN 978-1-4654-0888-4 (Library binding)
ISBN 978-1-4654-0887-7 (Hardcover)

DK books are available at special discounts when purchased in bulk
for sales promotions, premiums, fund-raising, or educational use. For
details, contact: DK Publishing Special Markets, 345 Hudson Street,
New York, New York 10014 or SpecialSales@dk.com.
Color reproduction by MDP, UK
Printed and bound in China by South China Printing Co. Ltd

Discover more at
www.dk.com

Ancient Greek wine cup

Statue of Gilgamesh,
legendary Mesopotamian king

Darius I, Persian king

Ancient Egyptian jars
containing a mummy's organs

Chavín bowl from
ancient Peru

Scarab pendant from
Tutankhamun's tomb

Contents

Roman theatrical masks

First steps to civilization

Historians call a society a "civilization" if it is complex and organized on lots of levels. In a civilization, some people live in cities—and perform a range of different jobs. Those in the countryside produce food in plenty, which provides enough wealth for city living. Everyone is ruled by a central government. As a civilization grows, people develop writing systems and new knowledge and skills, such as mathematics and law. A common form of money evolves, which is helpful in trade. Every civilization grows according to some patterns, but not in exactly the same way.

FARMING
Farming was the key development of all civilizations because it allowed people to settle in permanent villages. Like many early civilizations, the ancient Egyptians founded their society on the fertile banks of a river. Egypt's Nile River had rich soil on its banks that was ideal for growing crops.

CITY LIFE
As farming techniques improved and food production increased, early settlements grew larger and more complex. Gradually, they evolved into mighty cities with grand buildings, such as Athens in ancient Greece.

ART STYLES
Civilizations often developed their own distinct styles of art and architecture, which helped to unify the culture and give people a sense of belonging. Made from delicately crafted pieces of gold, glass, and semiprecious stones, this scarab (beetle) pendant, made for Pharaoh Tutankhamun, is typical of art styles in the time of ancient Egypt's New Kingdom.

The scarab was part of the religious beliefs of ancient Egypt

A city scene showing Athenians taking part in a public ritual in honor of Athena, their goddess

SOCIAL HIERARCHIES
Usually, the more complex a civilization got, the more unequal it became. Societies developed a series of levels, or a hierarchy, in which people's positions depended on their value to that society. This image shows the pyramid structure of Mayan society. There were always fewer people at the top of the social pyramid than at the bottom.

Mayan king

Members of the royal family

Nobles, priests, and warriors

Craftsmen

Farmers, laborers, and slaves

VARIETY OF JOBS
As agriculture developed, food became plentiful and all people in the society did not need to farm. Some became free to learn other skills—to make pottery, become construction workers, or create glass vessels, such as these ones from ancient Rome.

Statue of Athena

MAYAN KING
The people of each ancient civilization had shared beliefs and a shared religion. Priests usually enjoyed a high status, and in many civilizations, such as the Mayan, the rulers were also the religious leaders. This 8th-century stone carving shows the Mayan king Taj Chan Ahk taking part in a ceremony.

Model of an ancient Egyptian scribe

WRITING
The development of writing helped deal with the increasing complexity of civilizations because it made it possible to keep track of trade and government business. Scribes (professional writers) in the ancient world were skilled workers because most people could not read or write.

Digging up the past

Pyramid of the Niches, star attraction of El Tajín, cleared of rain-forest plants and soil in the 1930s

ARCHEOLOGISTS DISCOVER, dig up, and interpret the remains of past societies—the places where people lived, the objects they used, and any written records they may have kept. This is one of the main ways we learn about ancient civilizations. Archeology doesn't always provide a complete picture, however. It is usually only the hard objects, such as metals, pottery, and stone, that last, to be dug up by future generations. Softer materials, such as fabric, leather, and wood, rot away.

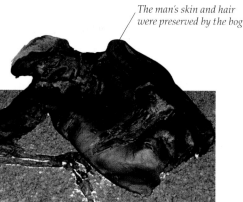

The man's skin and hair were preserved by the bog

ARCHEOLOGY
Archeologists are historians and scientists who excavate, or dig up, ancient sites and study the objects discovered to understand what they were and what they tell us about the people who once used them. Here we see archeologists working at the site of El Tajín in Mexico, which flourished in 600–1200 CE. Although archeologists first explored the site in the early 20th century, experts believe that only half of the site has been uncovered.

NATURAL PRESERVATION
The soft parts of people usually rot away, leaving just the skeleton. But certain natural environments can slow down the decaying process. This 2,000-year-old body of a man was found preserved in a peat bog in England.

Pickax

Brush

Dental pick

Plumb bob

TOOLS OF THE TRADE
Once soil has been removed by shovel and pickax, archeology is a task of precision. Archeologists use fine tools, such as soft brushes, dental picks, and tweezers, to carefully reveal and remove any artifacts (historical objects). To survey the land, they use the plumb bob—a weight that hangs at the end of a line and helps to check if something is perfectly vertical or not.

Sample of bone being collected for radiocarbon dating

Scientist wears gloves so as not to contaminate the artifact

DATING THE PAST

Archeologists use different clues to tell how old an artifact is. One of them is radiocarbon dating. In this process, they measure the amount of carbon-14 (a form of carbon) left in the remains of living things. In this image, a scientist is taking a small sample from a medieval human bone using a hand drill to find out how much carbon-14 it contains.

Tutankhamun's mummy, wrapped in bandages

PEERING INSIDE

To find out what is inside an ancient object—perhaps a sarcophagus with a mummy or a mummy wrapped in bandages—archeologists use a CT scan, which is a type of X-ray. The CT scanner builds up 3-D images from many X-ray "slices." When researchers put Tutankhamun's mummy through a CT scanner in 2005, they disproved a theory that the king had been killed by a blow to the head. They did find evidence that his leg had been broken before he died, and it may have led to his death.

Archeologist working at the site

HEINRICH SCHLIEMANN

The German archeologist Heinrich Schliemann was originally a businessman who taught himself archeology. He became one of the most famous archeologists of the 19th century, thanks to his excavation of many sites, including Troy and Mycenae. These two sites are associated with the Trojan War—an epic 10-year battle in which the Greeks used the famous Trojan Horse to invade Troy and win the war.

Mesopotamia
(3500–2000 BCE)

ONE OF THE WORLD'S OLDEST civilizations emerged in Mesopotamia—an area of the Middle East—in around 3500 BCE. Here, farmers had first settled on the flood plains of the Tigris and Euphrates rivers around 6000 BCE. They developed sophisticated forms of irrigation that allowed them to grow more crops and to turn their settlements into the first cities.

SUMER AND THE FIRST CITIES
Mud-brick villages were built in the 6th millennium BCE in a region called Sumer. From around 4300 BCE onward, these grew to become towns, and then the world's first cities. The population of the largest city, Uruk, may have been more than 50,000.

Early Mesopotamian cities

Wooden cross-piece holds planks together

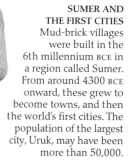

Lion

HISTORY MAKERS
The Mesopotamians were history's great pioneers. They came up with the idea for the wheel, which they first used to make pottery, later attaching it to vehicles. They traveled using the first sailboats and invented a system of writing, the science of mathematics, and even a calendar.

Replica of a simple three-part Mesopotamian wheel

KINGS AND PRIESTS
Each Sumerian city was ruled by a king, who was the head of the government, the leader of the army, and the chief priest. This statue shows Gilgamesh, a legendary king of Uruk who was part human and part god. The Sumerian *Epic of Gilgamesh*, from around 2000 BCE, tells of his many adventures and is one of the earliest recorded stories.

Statue of Gilgamesh from Khorsabad, Iraq, 8th century BCE

Chariot pulled
by donkeys

Soldiers armed
with spears

King of Ur, shown much
larger than other figures

Prisoners
of war

WEAPONS AND WARFARE

As they grew, Sumer's cities began to go to war over resources such as land and water. This led to the development of the first organized armies as well as new types of weapons. The Sumerians were among the first peoples to master bronze. This decorated panel from the city of Ur dates from around 2500 BCE and is one of the earliest representations of a Sumerian army.

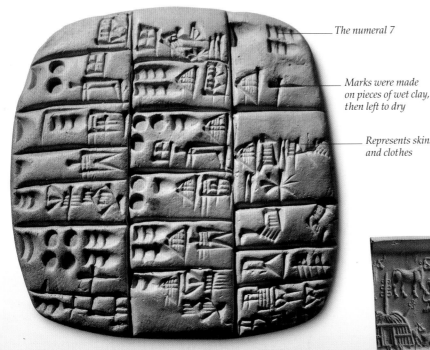

The numeral 7

Marks were made
on pieces of wet clay,
then left to dry

Represents skins
and clothes

THE FIRST WRITING

Some of the world's first traces of writing are Sumerian pictographs (picture writing), scratched on clay, from 3400 BCE. Over centuries, the Sumerians developed their picture script into cuneiform symbols (above), which were pressed into the clay as wedges and circles. They wrote in cuneiform to keep track of goods, possessions, and taxes, but later used it to write everything from official documents to stories. The tablet above is a list of goats and sheep.

SEALS FOR RECORD

The Sumerians marked their ownership of goods and documents by using cylinder seals. These were pieces of stone engraved with unique patterns. They were rolled onto tablets of wet clay, making an imprint. This marking acted as a signature, showing who owned what. Cylinder seals were also worn as jewelry and religious amulets.

Cattle surrounding
a building

Clay tablet

Cylinder seal from
4th millennium BCE

ZIGGURATS

By 2000 BCE, many Sumerian cities had large pyramid-shaped temples called ziggurats. This is a restored ziggurat in Ur. A ziggurat was the spiritual center of a city and was thought to be the earthly home of the gods. Later, the Assyrians and the Babylonians also built ziggurats.

Pschent or double crown | Scarab (beetle) stood for rebirth

Kingdoms of ancient Egypt
(3100 BCE–30 BCE)

Historians divide Egypt's 3,000-year-long ancient civilization into three main periods—the Old Kingdom, the Middle Kingdom, and the New Kingdom. These were the times when Egypt's power was at its height. In between came the "intermediate periods," when the state was weakened by civil wars, droughts, and invasions. Egypt's civilization declined in the 1st millennium BCE and was finally absorbed into the Roman Empire in 30 BCE.

EARLY EGYPT
Egyptian farming settlements, founded in around 5000 BCE, merged over the next 2,000 years to form two kingdoms—Upper Egypt in the south and Lower Egypt in the north. In 3100 BCE, Pharaoh Narmer unified the territory into a single state. His double crown, or Pschent, symbolized this union.

Nubian soldiers

OLD KINGDOM (2686–2181 BCE)
Egypt grew wealthy in this period as farming methods improved and food production increased. The pharaohs grew so powerful that they came to be regarded as godlike figures. They ordered giant statues, temples, and tombs, such as the pyramids of Giza, to be built in their honor. At the end of the Old Kingdom, however, a series of famines weakened the pharaohs' authority.

MIDDLE KINGDOM (2055–1650 BCE)
During this time, the pharaohs regained much of their prestige. They reclaimed some authority by conquering Nubia to the south. However, a Nubian revolt and an invasion by the Hyksos people to the north brought the Middle Kingdom to an end.

The Great Pyramid of Giza

CLEOPATRA VII
Cleopatra VII (reigned 51–30 BCE), Egypt's last pharaoh, was one of the few female rulers of the kingdom. To keep Egypt independent, she formed alliances with Julius Caesar and Mark Antony, the leaders of the region's new dominant power, Rome. After Antony's defeat in a Roman civil war, Cleopatra took her own life and Egypt became part of the Roman Empire.

NEW KINGDOM (1532–1070 BCE)
With the Hyksos forced out and Nubia reconquered, the pharaohs were in a commanding position again in the New Kingdom. One of the most powerful pharaohs, Ramses II (reigned 1279–1213 BCE) built an enormous temple filled with statues of himself at Abu Simbel (above). Much of Egypt's wealth was in the hands of priests and was used to build massive temples, such as the one at Abu Simbel. This wasted Egypt's resources and royal authority declined. Finally, in 712 BCE, Nubians sought their revenge and conquered Egypt.

Uraeus, a snake-shaped ornament

Sphinx built in honor of Pharaoh Khafra (reigned c. 2558–2532 BCE)

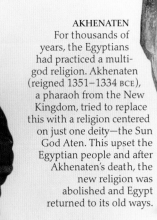

AKHENATEN
For thousands of years, the Egyptians had practiced a multi-god religion. Akhenaten (reigned 1351–1334 BCE), a pharaoh from the New Kingdom, tried to replace this with a religion centered on just one deity—the Sun God Aten. This upset the Egyptian people and after Akhenaten's death, the new religion was abolished and Egypt returned to its old ways.

Nefertiti, Akhenaten's wife   Akhenaten

Statue of Cleopatra VII

Hieroglyphics (formal script)

Demotic (everyday script)

LATE PERIOD
In the 1st millennium BCE, Egypt was taken over by a succession of foreign powers, including the Nubians, the Assyrians, the Persians, and, finally, the Greek forces of Alexander the Great. The new Greek rulers refused to learn Egyptian, so all official documents were written in both Egyptian and Greek.

Greek

Rosetta Stone, written in three scripts

Life in ancient Egypt

FROM HUMBLE FARMWORKERS to the pharaoh, everyone's life in ancient Egypt revolved around the cycles of the Nile River. The year was divided into three parts: flooding, sowing, and harvesting. Most of the population worked as farmers. Good harvests brought wealth to the land, which contributed to building Egypt's cities. The writing system helped to keep records of farm goods and cattle. However, the pharaoh and religion dominated Egypt's social life, with the gods playing a vital role in daily activities. The pharaoh also employed people to build temples and monuments.

THE NILE RIVER
The Nile wasn't vital for farming alone. The Egyptians used boats to fish its waters and to transport goods. On ceremonial occasions, pharaohs traveled in elaborate barges. The Egyptians also collected rushes called papyrus that grew on the river's edge to make mats, boats, papyrus paper, and other goods.

WRITING
By around 3000 BCE, the Egyptians had developed a writing system known as hieroglyphics (meaning "sacred writing") that used pictures to represent sounds and ideas. Used mainly for religious inscriptions, the hieroglyphs were complex and writing them took a long time.

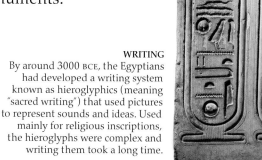

Name of Pharaoh Akhenaten (p. 13) spelled in hieroglyphics

Disk representing the Sun

Vulture's wing

EGYPTIAN GODS
The Egyptians had many different gods, whom they believed controlled the natural forces, such as Ra for the Sun, Thoth for the Moon, and Khnum for the Nile River. Osiris was the god of the afterlife. Gods were often depicted as being part animal and part human. Ma'at, the goddess of truth, is shown here with a human body and a vulture's wings.

Scribe counting the number of cattle

Farmer driving cattle with a stick

Cattle provided Egyptians with milk and meat

Falcon-headed Horus was the god of kingship

Jackal-headed Anubis was the god of embalming

PRIESTS
Although the pharaoh was Egypt's religious head, most of the day-to-day rituals that were designed to keep the gods happy were performed by priests. Priests were often important government officials. Sometimes, the chief priest held the role of vizier, the most powerful figure after the pharaoh. The priests carried standards, or poles, in their processions and used bronze containers that held holy water from a sacred lake.

Copper standard

Sacred bucket for holy water

SUPREME RULER
The pharaoh was the supreme ruler of ancient Egyptian society, regarded as being half man and half god. His, or sometimes her, word was law. The pharaoh was in charge of the army and the government and, as Egypt's religious leader, also provided a link between the ordinary people and the gods.

Pharaoh Ramses I (reigned 1295–1294 BCE) flanked by the gods Horus and Anubis

TEMPLES
Every Egyptian town had a temple where a particular god was worshiped. The Egyptians believed the god lived inside the temple in the form of a statue. Only pharaohs and priests were allowed into the inner temple where the statue was situated. Special temples, known as mortuary temples, were built as places where deceased pharaohs were worshiped.

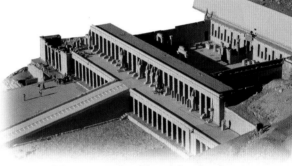

Mortuary temple of Egypt's female ruler, Pharaoh Hatshepsut (reigned c. 1473–1458 BCE)

ORDINARY EGYPTIANS
Pharaohs lived in stone palaces, dressed in the finest clothes, and enjoyed the best food. Most Egyptians, however, lived simple lives as farmers, field hands, fishermen, craftsworkers, artists, and tradespeople. They lived in mud-brick houses, ate a diet of bread and porridge made from grain, and wore simple linen clothes.

Meketre, government official and owner of cattle

Meketre's son

Tomb model showing an everyday scene of cattle counting

Afterlife in ancient Egypt

THE AFTERLIFE was just as important to the ancient Egyptians as their life on Earth. In fact, they spent much of their lives preparing for what they believed would happen after death. To get to the afterlife, the Egyptians believed three things were necessary: they had to have their names written down somewhere; their bodies had to be mummified; and they had to live a good life so that their hearts were free of sin.

Mummy of Pharaoh Seti II (reigned 1200–1194 BCE) wrapped in linen

MUMMIFICATION
Mummifying a body took around 70 days. First, the internal organs were removed. The brain was pulled out through the nose with a hook and thrown away because it was considered useless. Only the heart was left behind because the Egyptians believed it was the source of all thought and emotion. The body was then dried, wrapped in linen strips, and placed in its coffin.

CANOPIC JARS
The removed organs were placed in special jars in the tomb, each with a lid representing a particular god. Imnesty (a human's head) was for the liver, Duamutef (a jackal's head) for the stomach, Hapy (a baboon's head) for the lungs, and Qebehsenuf (a falcon's head) for the intestines.

JUDGING THE DEAD
According to Egyptian mythology, the god Anubis weighed the deceased's heart against the "feather of truth." If the heart was light and free of sin, the person entered the afterlife. If it was heavy with sin, it was eaten by a monster named Ammut the Devourer and the deceased was gone forever.

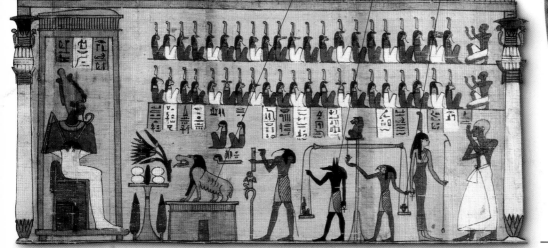

Ammut the Devourer   *Anubis*   *Heart being weighed*

Cobra

A STEP TO A PYRAMID
Early pharaohs were buried in single-story stone tombs known as mastabas. From this came the idea of building a step pyramid by placing mastabas of decreasing size one on top of the other. The first smooth-sided pyramids were created under Pharaoh Sneferu (reigned 2613–2589 BCE).

Early Egyptian pyramids were step pyramids

Pyramid of Djoser (reigned 2667–2648 BCE)

Cap stone

GREAT PYRAMID
Pyramids grew larger as the Old Kingdom went on, reaching a peak with the creation of Pharaoh Khufu's Great Pyramid at Giza. Completed in around 2560 BCE and standing 481 ft (146.5 m) tall, it is the tallest stone structure ever built that is still standing. It is made up of some two million stone blocks.

Pharaoh's burial chamber

Abandoned burial chamber

Original burial chamber

Exterior, originally covered in smooth limestone

VALLEY OF THE KINGS
Pyramids were magnificent statements of power, but they were easy to find and were eventually looted by grave robbers. To prevent this, the pharaohs of the New Kingdom were buried in secret underground tombs in a place called the Valley of the Kings. Most of these tombs were also robbed, but one belonging to Pharaoh Tutankhamun (reigned 1336–1327 BCE) lay undetected until 1922. It was filled with treasures, including jewelry and the pharaoh's death mask.

Necklace found in Tutankhamun's tomb

Tutankhamun's gold death mask

Indus Valley civilization
(2600–1800 BCE)

THE RISE OF THE INDUS CIVILIZATION followed a similar pattern to the emergence of the first civilization in Mesopotamia. People began farming the floodplains of the Indus River around 4000 BCE, building a network of canals to supply water to the fields. Towns appeared around 3000 BCE, and by 2600 BCE, the floodplains were filled with sophisticated cities, some with populations of many thousands. Following the Indus cities' decline in around 1800 BCE, a new mighty civilization took root to the east in the Ganges valley that went on to dominate most of northern India.

RIVER VALLEY CITIES
The Indus civilization was spread across a huge area of modern Afghanistan, Pakistan, and northwest India. At its peak, around 2500 BCE, there were more than 2,000 towns scattered across the plains. Harappa and Mohenjo-daro were the largest of them. Harappa's population was around 25,000, while Mohenjo-daro's was around 40,000.

TOWN PLANNING
Indus towns were laid out in a grid pattern—the wide roads divided them in rectangular or square blocks. They were packed with mud-brick buildings, many of which were several stories high. The Indus people were masters of water management. Many houses had wells for drinking water and drains to take away dirty water, and some even had toilets—the first in the world. The image below shows the Great Bath, 7¾ ft (2.4 m) deep, at the center of Mohenjo-daro.

ARTS AND CRAFTS
The craftspeople of the Indus civilization were just as skilled as the builders. They used wheels to create clay pots, which were decorated with paintings of nature. They made delicate items of jewelry from shells and stones and often buried these in the graves of high-ranking individuals. They also cast statues, such as this bronze figure of a dancing girl, shown wearing a necklace and bracelets that cover one arm.

Dancing girl

Seals found as far away as Mesopotamia show that the Indus people traded widely.

Most seals had an image of an animal

WRITING

More than 3,500 small, square clay seals have been recovered from Indus towns. Decorated with complex symbols and pictures, they show that the people had developed a writing system. The seals were probably used to mark ownership of goods, but since historians have not yet been able to interpret the script, we cannot be certain.

TRANSPORTATION

Wheels were not just used for spinning pots. The Indus was one of the first civilizations to develop wheeled vehicles. Although no remains of Indus vehicles have been found (they were probably made of wood, which would have rotted away), clay models of toy carts, such as this one, have been discovered. Some Indus roads have deep ruts that experts believe were made by wheeled traffic.

METALWORKERS

Indus metalworkers used silver, gold, lead, tin, bronze, and copper, which was the most common metal. Copper was used to create both intricate pieces of jewelry and weapons, such as spearheads.

Copper spearheads

Bulls pulling a two-wheeled cart

Sculpted toy chariot recovered from Mohenjo-daro

Raised area known as the citadel, where the rulers probably lived

THE END OF INDUS

The Indus civilization began to decline in 1900–1800 BCE. A late Harappan culture existed until around 1300 BCE, with typical red clay pottery, but most of the cities disappeared or were abandoned. The reasons for this are unclear, partly because the Indus writing system, which may have provided some clues, cannot be understood. It is thought that climate change may have made farming difficult because it changed the cycle of floods and seasonal monsoons. This may have forced the people to leave the towns and cities.

Late Harappan red clay burial pot

GANGES CIVILIZATION

After the Indus cities declined, the people in north India returned to rural living. Around 1500 BCE, another urban civilization emerged in India. Nomads, or people who wandered from place to place, came from central Asia and began settling around the Ganges River. Over time, these settlements grew into 16 large kingdoms known as Mahajanapadas. Two major religious beliefs—Hinduism and Buddhism—appeared in this period. This mural at a temple in Thailand shows Prince Siddhartha Gautama (c. 563–483 BCE), whose teachings were the principles of Buddhism.

Eighteenth-century CE mural depicting Prince Siddhartha leaving his royal life

Bronze Age and Iron Age Europe

The Bronze Age began when people learned to extract copper from rock and mix it with tin to produce an alloy (mixed metal) called bronze. The technology emerged in western Asia around 3600 BCE and spread through Europe from 2500 BCE. European societies, especially their tools, became more sophisticated with the use of bronze. The next leap forward came with the coming of iron, which was harder and cheaper than bronze. This began in western Asia around 1500 BCE and spread through Europe in 1200–500 BCE. During the Iron Age, the Celtic culture flourished in Europe. Many Celts in modern France, Germany, and Britain were eventually conquered by the Roman Empire.

BEFORE BRONZE

Tools of early European cultures were made of stone and bone. However, Europeans were able to build religious sites made from large stones called megaliths using these tools. Eventually, stone tools gave way to copper ones, and, in time, bronze ones.

Prehistoric copper tool from Italy

Gilded disk believed to represent the Sun

HALLSTATT CELTS

The earliest Celtic culture was the Hallstatt Culture of central Europe. The culture began around 1200 BCE and the Hallstatt people began to use iron tools around 800 BCE. A new Celtic culture, the La Tène Culture, replaced the Hallstatt Culture around 450 BCE and spread across central and western Europe.

THE ARRIVAL OF BRONZE

The first people to use bronze in Europe lived in what is now Poland. As skills improved, elaborate arts and crafts flourished across Europe, as seen in this Sun Chariot. By 1400 BCE, a distinct civilization known as the Urnfield Culture emerged, which has been named after the pots, or urns, in which they buried the ashes of their dead.

Bronze buckle from Hallstatt Culture

Bronze horse stands on four wheels

Bronze Age model of Sun Chariot from 1800–1600 BCE, discovered in Trundholm, Denmark

CELTIC VILLAGES

Although the Celts are well-known for their warlike character, they spent most of their time farming and hunting. They did not, however, develop one style of architecture across all Celtic territory. Instead, they built according to the local conditions. In Britain's lowlands, they made round houses with timber frames and thatched roofs, such as these reconstructed ones in Castell Henllys, Wales. Wood was used because it was widely available and the roofs kept in the warmth.

Maiden Castle, an Iron Age hill fort of the Celts, southern England

TRIBES AND FORTS

The Celts lived in tribes headed by a chieftain, who organized the building of hilltop forts defended by deep ditches, such as this one in Britain. These weren't, however, strong enough to keep out the Roman army, which eventually conquered most of the Celts' territory.

WEAPONS AND WARFARE

Celts used their mastery of bronze and iron to create a range of weapons, including swords, spears, javelins, and daggers, which they used in the wars among the tribes. They also fashioned iron helmets, war trumpets, and shields.

Celtic bronze shield from 2nd–1st century BCE

Celtic bronze sword and scabbard from 8th century BCE

Minoans and Mycenaeans
(2700–1250 BCE)

THE MINOANS, who founded Europe's first civilization, emerged on the Greek island of Crete in around 2700 BCE. They traded widely with the region's other peoples, using the wealth accumulated to build lavish palaces. The civilization eventually declined, and in the 15th century BCE, the Mycenaeans from mainland Greece took over Crete. The Mycenaeans thrived for several hundred years before being overrun by foreign invaders.

RISE OF CRETE
In the early 2nd millennium BCE, Crete was divided into a number of prosperous kingdoms, including Phaistos, Malia, and Knossos. At around the same time, the Mycenaean civilization was growing on mainland Greece.

Legendary hero Theseus killing the minotaur

Bull's head

Statue of Theseus and the minotaur from 19th century CE

Dolphin fresco at Knossos

KNOSSOS
Around 1700 BCE, many Minoan palaces were destroyed, possibly by fire. Over the next few centuries, one palace, Knossos, recovered its splendour and continued to grow, becoming the largest palace on the island of Crete. It boasted hundreds of rooms, many of which were decorated with beautiful frescoes.

DISASTER STRIKES
In addition to expanding Knossos, the Minoans also established a number of overseas colonies on other Greek islands. One of these, Akrotiri on Thera (now known as Santorini), was buried beneath a river of lava in 1628 BCE following a huge volcanic eruption— one of the largest in human history.

Jars found at Akrotiri

LEGEND OF THE MINOTAUR
After the Minoan civilization vanished, the Greeks invented many fantastical stories about its people. These included the legend of the minotaur, a half-man, half-bull monster who lived in a vast maze called the labyrinth. The story was probably inspired by the large, mazelike Minoan palaces and because Minoans considered bulls to be sacred.

RISE OF MYCENAE

The people who founded the Mycenaean civilization arrived in mainland Greece, possibly from Turkey, around 2500 BCE. By 2000 BCE, a number of small kingdoms had been established, each ruled by a king from a hilltop fortress known as a citadel. The most important citadel was Mycenae itself, and one of its best-known kings was Agamemnon. This mask was once thought to be his.

Mycenaean gold jewelry depicting a female figure

METAL MASTERS

The Mycenaeans were skilled metalworkers, fashioning bronze weapons, which they used to conquer Crete in the 15th century BCE. They also put their talents to more peaceful uses, creating intricate, delicate items from gold.

Gold funeral mask, Mycenae, 16th century BCE

A modern reconstruction of the Trojan horse

TRADE AND EXPANSION

The Mycenaeans took over and expanded the trade routes of the Minoans. They continued trade in agricultural produce, such as olive oil and wine, as well as craft objects. However, they extended their power further through war, leading raids against Egypt and the Hittite people of Turkey.

Olives and olive oil are still produced in Greece today

FALL OF MYCENAE

From 1200 BCE onward, the Mycenaean citadels were abandoned, perhaps following an attack from foreign raiders known as the "sea peoples." But the Greeks continued to tell the mythical story of the Trojan War, an epic 10-year battle between Mycenae and Troy (in modern Turkey). The Mycenaeans won by smuggling soldiers into Troy in a giant wooden horse.

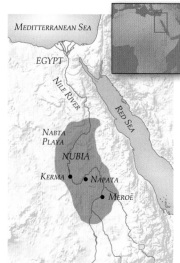

Nubia
(2000 BCE–200 BCE)

THE NUBIAN CULTURE EMERGED around 5000 BCE on the banks of the Nile River at around the same time the Egyptians were laying down roots farther north. The Nubian civilization developed around 2000 BCE. Egypt and Nubia became rivals, with Egypt invading Nubia at intervals and enslaving its people in 2040–1640 BCE. The Nubians, however, fought back, ejecting the Egyptians. They even took over Egypt in 730 BCE and ruled the two kingdoms briefly.

EARLY NUBIA
In its early period, the Nubian civilization was probably more advanced than the Egyptian. At a place called Nabta Playa, the Nubians erected complex arrangements of stones, which may have been the world's earliest astronomical device. By the end of the Old Kingdom in 2181 BCE, however, Egypt was the Nile's dominant power.

Model of Nubian soldiers from Egypt's Middle Kingdom

KERMA
Nubia emerged from Egypt's shadow following the fall of the Old Kingdom, and the first Nubian kingdom developed around the city of Kerma. But during Egypt's powerful Middle Kingdom, Pharaoh Senusret I conquered Lower Nubia in 1965 BCE. Under Egypt's rule, the Nubian soldiers served in the Egyptian army. Well-known for their expertise, Nubian archers were greatly valued by the Egyptians. Later, when the Hyksos people from the Levant invaded Egypt, it was the cue for Nubians to revolt and reestablish control of Lower Nubia.

Nubian archer armed with bows and arrows —————

NEW KINGDOM NUBIA
In the New Kingdom, Egypt reasserted its dominance. Kerma was sacked by Pharaoh Tuthmosis I and the Egyptians took over Lower Nubia. Pharaoh Ramses II underlined Egypt's authority by building a vast temple complex at Abu Simbel, in what had been part of Nubia. This was adorned with giant statues of the pharaoh.

Pharaoh Tuthmosis I

Nubian merchant

TRADING TIES
Relations between Egypt and Nubia weren't always hostile. For most of their history, the two civilizations interacted through trade. Nubia had many natural resources, including gold mines, and the Nubians were in contact with the cultures of tropical Africa, which gave them access to ivory and animal skins. They traded these for Egyptian artifacts and craft goods.

Nubian merchants arrive in Egypt with boats filled with animal skins and ivory

Nubian prisoner   *Ramses II*

NUBIANS MOVE TO KUSH
In the face of attacks by the Egyptians under Ramses II and others, the Nubians withdrew farther south, establishing a new kingdom, Kush. Despite their conflicts, the two civilizations were culturally close, and around 730 BCE, the Nubian ruler Piye merged the two cultures, conquering Egypt.

Gold bracelet from Meroë

MOVE TO MEROË
The Nubians' rule of Egypt lasted less than a century before the Egyptians drove them out again. The Nubian capital, Napata, was sacked, forcing the Nubians farther south to form a new kingdom at Meroë. Here, a more distinctly Nubian culture thrived, and unlike Egypt, Nubia successfully fended off a Roman invasion.

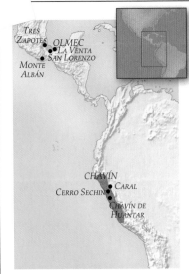

America's first civilizations
(2600 BCE–200 BCE)

FROM THE 3RD MILLENNIUM BCE ONWARD, new civilizations started developing in two very different areas of the Americas. In the lowlands of Mesoamerica—the area corresponding to modern-day Mexico and Central America—the Olmecs became experts in growing corn, which went on to become the region's main crop, and built great ceremonial centers. At around the same time, people living on the coasts and in the mountains of Peru in South America were becoming skilled in fishing and farming.

RISE OF THE AMERICAS
The Olmec civilization emerged on the river floodplains of southern Mexico in around 2000 BCE. At around the same time, but thousands of miles south, the older cultures that created the urban centers of Caral, the first in the Americas, and Cerro Sechin, were also growing.

CERRO SECHIN
The first complex societies in South America were based not on farming, but on fishing the rich waters of the Peruvian coast. With the development of farming in the 2nd millennium BCE, the civilization spread inland. Cerro Sechin was one of the main urban centers of the time. Scenes of battles and warriors adorning its temples suggest it lay at the heart of a warlike society.

Cerro Sechin engraving of a warrior holding a club, 1st millennium BCE

Giant Olmec head from La Venta

OLMEC CULTURE
Sometimes called the "mother culture of Mesoamerica," the Olmec culture had many features, such as pyramid building, playing ball games, and bloodletting—a ritual in which people cut or pierced a part of their bodies. These continued to be practiced by societies that flourished later in the region. The Olmecs also created highly distinctive art, often featuring a half-human, half-feline creature known as the were-jaguar (left).

URBAN CENTERS

By 1200 BCE, the Olmecs had established San Lorenzo as their main ceremonial center. Around 900 BCE, however, San Lorenzo was destroyed and replaced with a larger center, La Venta. The Olmecs moved again around 400 BCE to a third center, Tres Zapotes. But the civilization was already in decline by this time and faded away soon afterward.

LAND OF THE GIANT HEADS

In addition to carving small, delicate jade figurines, the Olmecs also worked at the opposite end of the scale, fashioning giant stone heads of their leaders that adorned their ceremonial centers. Carved out of volcanic rock, the biggest heads are over 10 ft (3 m) tall and weigh more than 50 tons.

Jade figures from La Venta performing a sacred ritual

THE ZAPOTECS

A new culture, partly based on Olmec traditions, emerged to the west of the Olmec heartland around 400 BCE. At their capital, Monte Albán, the Zapotecs also built pyramids and created art that mixed human and animal forms, such as this clay sculpture showing a god emerging from the mouth of a jaguar.

Ears of corn, the Zapotecs' main food, frame the god's face

Sculpture of a Zapotec god

THE CHAVÍN

From 800 BCE onward, Peru's dominant culture became the Chavín. Chavín people adapted well to the mountainous terrain, farming the land using terraces and building the large ceremonial center of Chavín de Huántar. They were also skilled craftspeople, creating intricate pottery, such as this animal-shaped bowl.

Chavín pottery

Ancient China
(2000 BCE–220 CE)

By the time the first emperor of China came to the throne in 221 BCE, Chinese civilization had been flourishing for several thousand years. The rigid, centralized government that the emperor created was passed on to a series of dynasties, or ruling families, who controlled power until 1912. The ancient Chinese came up with numerous world-changing inventions such as paper, silk, cast iron, the crossbow, and the seismometer (earthquake detector).

EARLY CULTURES
The Chinese civilization emerged in the fertile valley of the Yellow River. Here, first the Yangshao Culture (5000 BCE onward) and then the Longshan Culture (3000 BCE onward) flourished. The people farmed the land and produced intricate pieces of pottery.

SHANG AND ZHOU
In the 2nd millennium BCE, Chinese civilization grew in sophistication under the Shang Dynasty. People mastered the art of casting bronze, as shown by this ritual bronze vessel. The Shang ruled from around 1600 BCE until 1027 BCE, when they were overthrown by the Zhou Dynasty.

Dragon's body covered with fish scales

MYTHICAL CREATURE
In Chinese mythology, dragons were not monsters, but helpful creatures that symbolized strength and wisdom. To associate themselves with the same qualities, Chinese emperors adopted the dragon as their symbol.

Golden imperial dragon

Qin Shi
Huangdi

TERRA-COTTA ARMY
Qin Shi Huangdi unified China by dealing ruthlessly with his enemies so no one could challenge his power. He even made sure he was protected in the afterlife and had himself buried with the Terra-cotta Army—thousands of life-sized clay figures, including soldiers with metal weapons. The system of government he established lasted for more than 2,000 years.

Face made with mold

THE FIRST EMPEROR
The Zhou kingdom eventually split into separate states that went to war in 480 BCE. Each wanted to establish its control across China. The leader of the state of Qin, King Zheng (reigned 246–210 BCE), won the conflict. Zheng gave himself a new name, Qin Shi Huangdi, which means "first emperor."

HAN DYNASTY (206 BCE–220 CE)
The Han Dynasty, which came after the Qin Dynasty, was formed by Liu Bang (reigned 206–195 BCE). Chinese economy and culture grew during the Han period. The Han people established the famous trade route called the Silk Road and invented paper. Artists painted beautiful murals on palace walls, and craftsmen made glazed pottery decorated with natural features, such as clouds and animals.

A soldier figure from the Terra-cotta Army

Cloud painted with red lacquer on Han Dynasty pottery

The Ming-built structure is the longest wall ever built, stretching for 3,890 miles (6,260 km)

Guards looked out for invaders from watchtowers built along the wall

THE GREAT WALL
Qin Shi Huangdi was a cruel ruler who forced slaves to build roads and canals across his empire, as well as erect his palace and tomb at the capital, Xi'an. To prevent an invasion, he also ordered a great earthen wall to be built across the north of China. A stone version of this wall was constructed in the 15th century CE during the Ming Dynasty.

Writing

Writing developed separately in different parts of the world as civilizations became more complex. It allowed people to make a note of who owned what, the debts people had, and paid or unpaid taxes. Over time, writing became more advanced and was used not just to record things, but also to express ideas and tell stories. As with civilization itself, the story of writing begins with the Sumerian people of Mesopotamia.

CUNEIFORM

The first writing system—a system of pictures called pictographic script—developed in Sumeria in around 3400 BCE. Over centuries, the pictures scratched on wet clay evolved into cuneiform—symbols built from wedges made by pressing a reed stylus (pen) into the clay. People were using cuneiform by 2900 BCE.

Solid blocks of ink

Grinder to crush pigments used to make ink

Egyptian stone ink holder

HIEROGLYPHICS

Around 3100 BCE, not long after the Sumerians created pictographs, the Egyptians developed their own form of writing, called hieroglyphics. The Egyptians carved symbols onto the walls of their buildings using copper chisels and painted them onto papyrus paper with reed pens. Colored inks were made from a variety of substances, including charcoal (black), clay (red and yellow), and copper (blue).

Hieroglyphs on papyrus from the Book of the Dead of an ancient Egyptian nobleman

Oxen

Reed pens

EUROPEAN BEGINNINGS

The earliest European writing system was hieroglyphics created by the Minoan people of Crete in the early 2nd millennium BCE. It wasn't the only system used. Minoans also created the mysterious symbols found only on this disk. They also wrote with simpler symbols in a system archeologists call Linear A. None of their writing has ever been deciphered.

These symbols on a clay disk from Crete are from a unique Minoan script

Phaistos disk, c. 1900 BCE

CHINESE WRITING

The Chinese came up with a pictographic writing system during the Shang Dynasty (1600–1046 BCE). The modern Chinese writing system, made up of thousands of symbols, developed under the Zhou Dynasty (1046–256 BCE).

Symbol for woman (left) and man (right)

Brushes and ink used for writing Chinese symbols

A scribe's wooden palette with holes for ink

Text has been written on palm leaves

INDIAN WRITING

Writing was developed twice in India. The first system was of the Indus civilization (pp. 18–19) and has not been interpreted yet. The second system, of the Ganges civilization (p. 19), was used to write Sanskrit. The earliest Hindu holy books in the 1st millennium BCE were written in Sanskrit.

Illustrated Sanskrit text from the 11th century CE

Each glyph represents a different word, sound, or number

MESOAMERICAN WRITING

Blocks of stone carved with symbols that may be a form of writing have been recovered from Olmec areas. These show that Olmecs were perhaps the first people in the Americas to develop writing. The people of the next major civilization, the Maya, used around 750 symbols, called glyphs, to write.

Mayan glyphs carved on a 6th-century CE stone slab

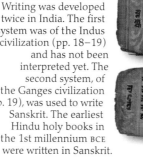

Greek writing based on the Canaanite alphabet

Names written on pottery pieces used during a vote by the people of Athens

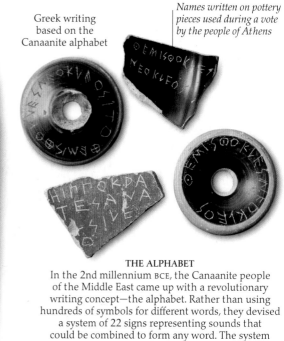

THE ALPHABET

In the 2nd millennium BCE, the Canaanite people of the Middle East came up with a revolutionary writing concept—the alphabet. Rather than using hundreds of symbols for different words, they devised a system of 22 signs representing sounds that could be combined to form any word. The system was later adopted by the Greeks.

The Phoenicians (1200–146 BCE)

BETWEEN 1200 AND 800 BCE, the Phoenician people used their sailing skills to establish a great trading network from their home in the Levant region across the Mediterranean. But they didn't just exchange goods. The Phoenicans were the news service of their day, spreading learning, culture, religious beliefs, and writing systems across the ancient world. They founded numerous cities, one of which, Carthage, went on to build a mighty empire.

PHOENICIAN CITY-STATES
Phoenicia was not an empire, but rather a loose association of city-states that gradually spread across the Mediterranean as trade expanded. The most important were Byblos, Sidon, and Tyre in modern Lebanon, and Carthage in North Africa. The highlighted areas on the map show Phoenician territories.

Sail raised in windy weather, increasing speed of boat

Mast held a single sail

SPREADING THE WORD
The cultural exchanges of the Phoenicians were of great benefit to civilization. The Phoenicians were the descendants of the Canaanites, who developed the world's first alphabet. The Greeks adopted it from the Phoenicians, made some improvements, such as adding vowels, and passed it on to the Romans. It is still used for many modern-day languages, including English.

The letter "G"

Tablet with Phoenician alphabet

Rigging to hold mast in place

Upper deck carried second row of oarsmen

SEAFARING PEOPLE
As they strived to open up new markets, the Phoenicians became the greatest sailors of the age and were one of the first peoples to sail out of sight of land. Master shipbuilders, they invented a new, fast vessel, called a bireme, powered by two decks of rowers and a sail. The boats were widely copied across the Mediterranean.

Battering ram to attack enemy boats

THE COLOR PURPLE
Of all the goods traded
by the Phoenicians, the one
that brought the biggest rewards
wasn't gold or silver, but a purple
dye made by boiling *Murex* sea snails.
Known as Tyrian purple, after the city
of Tyre, it was hugely expensive—it took
thousands of snails to make a small amount
of dye. This highly prized dye was the color
associated with the emperor in Rome.

Cloth dyed in purple

Murex shell

Ruins of Leptis Magna, once part of Carthaginian Empire

CARTHAGE
One of the city-states
founded by the Phoenicians,
Carthage in North Africa
grew extremely rich,
ruling a powerful empire
from the 6th century BCE
onward. At its height, the
Carthaginian Empire
covered much of
North Africa, parts
of Spain, and the
Italian islands of
Sicily and Sardinia.

Braces to hold the sail at right angle to the wind

HANNIBAL AND THE PUNIC WARS
In the 3rd and 2nd centuries BCE, Carthage
fought the three Punic Wars with Rome for
control of the Mediterranean. Although the
Carthaginians won several battles under their great
general Hannibal, they were eventually defeated.

Hannibal, the Carthaginian general

Shields of warriors to protect the oarsmen

Main hull made from a single tree trunk

TRADE GOODS
This 4th-century BCE glass
pendant was one of the
many goods traded by
the Phoenicians. The lack of
unity among the trading cities,
however, ultimately cost them
their independence as they
were taken over by the region's
other powers. Following the
rise of Alexander the Great,
Phoenicia was absorbed
into the Hellenistic world—
the Greek-dominated
world he established.

Steering oars

The Maya
(1200 BCE–1697 CE)

THE NEXT GREAT CIVILIZATION to arise in Mesoamerica after the Olmecs was the Maya. This civilization was at its peak during 300–800 CE, when dozens of great cities were erected and sophisticated systems of writing, mathematics, and astronomy were devised. It declined after this point—perhaps because of the overuse of land for farming—but there were still several Mayan cities remaining when Spanish invaders arrived in the 16th century. The last Mayan city fell to the Spanish in 1697.

GULF OF MEXICO

CHICHEN ITZA

PALENQUE • •TIKAL

PACIFIC OCEAN

MAYAN CITIES
Mayan cities, such as Palenque, Tikal, and Chichen Itza, were stretched out across a large area now occupied by southeastern Mexico, Belize, Guatemala, and Honduras. Each had its own ruler. The cities never joined together to form a single empire.

Large earplug

Hand holding jar

MAYAN GODS
This image shows Chaac, the Mayan god of rain, one of the many gods who were believed to control the forces of the natural world. Priests performed ceremonies for the gods to keep them happy. The Maya thought the world was divided into three parts— the Heavens, the Earth, and the Underworld, which were linked together by a giant "World Tree."

Bars and dots are Mayan glyphs for numbers

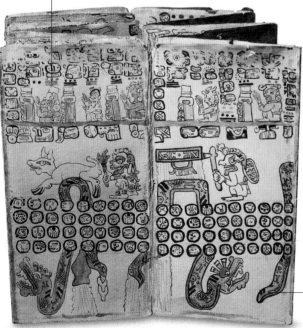

ARTS, CRAFTS, AND WRITING
The Maya were highly skilled artists and craftspeople, creating pottery, sculptures, and jewelry from jade, which they considered to be the most valuable of all materials. They also devised a writing system using symbols, called glyphs, for sounds and words. They carved glyphs onto stone slabs, called stelae, to record events, and also used them to make books. These books, known as codices, were made from thin pieces of bark and told stories about the Mayan gods.

Glyphs painted onto bark paper coated with fine layer of gesso (plaster of Paris)

Gods were often shown wearing elaborate headdresses

FARMING AND FOOD
Corn was the staple food of all Mesoamerican civilizations, including the Maya. It was considered so important that the Maya worshiped a god of corn and even believed that humans had originally been created from corn dough. The Maya also grew squash, sweet potatoes, beans, chiles, and other vegetables.

Squash

Sweet potato

Chiles

Corn

This band shows 20 days

Ball of incense

Priest performed rituals on top of the pyramids

ASTRONOMY
The Maya were skilled astronomers who carefully studied the sky because they believed the movements and positions of celestial bodies revealed the plans of the gods. Events, such as festivals or wars, were planned around celestial positions. They used their studies to devise calendars, which were adopted by later Mesoamerican civilizations. This reconstructed Aztec calendar is one such example.

GIANT CITIES
Mayan cities were always built according to the same pattern. At the center was the palace of the ruler, a plaza for the marketplace, and several giant pyramid temples where religious rituals and human sacrifices to the gods were performed. Tikal in Guatemala, one of the biggest Mayan cities, may have had as many as 60,000 inhabitants.

Mayan pyramid, Tikal

Assyria and Babylon
(1900–539 BCE)

ASSYRIA AND BABYLON emerged as important powers in Mesopotamia in 2000–1800 BCE, following the demise of Sumer. At times in the next 1,500 years they were fierce rivals. At its high point in the 600s BCE, the Assyrian Empire included both Egypt and Babylon. But Babylon fought back, taking control of Assyria and expanding its power throughout the region. Eventually, the Persian Empire took over both Babylon and Assyria.

ASSYRIAN EXPANSION
Assyria was at its peak in the 7th century BCE, when it took control of Babylon. Assyrians built an empire stretching across the Middle East, including Judah, Phoenicia, and Egypt. This map shows the Assyrian Empire at its greatest extent.

HAMMURABI
Founded in 1894 BCE, Babylon became a powerful city-state under King Hammurabi (reigned 1792–1750 BCE). To control his people, he created a code of laws, which was carved on this stone pillar and on clay tablets that have been found throughout his kingdom.

IVORY FROM AFRICA
The Assyrians built several large cities, including Ashur (the origin of the word Assyria), Nimrud, and Nineveh. These cities were home to great royal palaces, filled with treasures from across the empire, such as this ivory carving. Assyria got ivory (which comes from elephants' tusks) from Africa, showing the wide extent of Assyrian trade.

Hammurabi's law code carved onto a stone pillar

Ashurbanipal hunting with a bow and arrow

CONQUERING ARMIES
The Assyrian army consisted of thousands of soldiers and was greatly feared. In around 1000 BCE, it became one of the first to use iron weapons, which gave it a tremendous advantage over the region's other states, since most of them were still using bronze weapons, which were softer. The Assyrian king Ashurbanipal, etched on this carving from a palace at Nineveh, was the conqueror of Egypt.

Bucket and pulley system draws water from wells up to top level

Canals connected to wells to feed the plants

Tumbling waterfall

An artist's view of what the Hanging Gardens of Babylon may have looked like and details it may have contained.

THE HANGING GARDENS

Assyria's dominance did not last forever. It was replaced in the late 7th century BCE by the Babylonian Empire, which grew powerful under the rule of Nebuchadnezzar II (reigned 605–562 BCE). He is famed for building a spectacular complex of hanging gardens, which were named one of the Seven Wonders of the Ancient World. The remains of the gardens have not been found.

Canal feeding the gardens with water

Horses driving two-wheeled chariots

THE CITY OF BABYLON

Nebuchadnezzar II began a massive building program, ensuring that Babylon became the region's finest city. It was surrounded by walls with eight huge gates, the most spectacular of which was the Ishtar Gate. However, Babylon's independence was short-lived. Babylon was conquered by Persia in 539 BCE, shortly after Nebuchadnezzar's death.

Images of dragons and bulls decorate the gate

Modern recreation of the Ishtar Gate

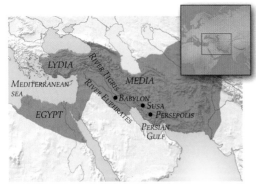

The Persian Empire
(550–334 BCE)

WHEN CYRUS II came to the throne in 559 BCE, his kingdom, Persis, was a minor state controlled by the much larger Median Empire. Over the next 30 years, he conquered all the major powers of the Middle East, creating the largest empire yet seen. His successors extended Persian territory farther. However, the empire fell to Alexander the Great's armies in 334 BCE.

RISE OF PERSIA
In the early 6th century BCE, the Middle East was dominated by four major powers—Media, Babylon, Egypt, and Lydia. By the end of the century, all four were under the control of Persia. This map shows the extent of the empire under the Persian king Darius I.

PERSEPOLIS
Persia's capital and greatest city was Persepolis, which was founded in around 515 BCE. It was built as a statement of Persian power. At its center was the vast Apadana Palace—its walls adorned with carvings of bulls and lions—which was designed to inspire awe in all who visited.

Statue of a griffin, a mythical creature with the head of an eagle and the body of a lion

Cuneiform script on clay cylinder tells of Cyrus's many achievements

CYRUS THE GREAT
Despite launching many wars, Cyrus II (reigned 559–530 BCE) had a reputation as a fair ruler who respected the beliefs and customs of those he conquered. Following his conquest of the Babylonian Empire, he allowed the Jews to return to their homeland from which they had been expelled by the Babylonians.

79-ft- (24-m-) high columns supported the palace

Persian gold earring from around 500 BCE

Ahura Mazda

ZOROASTRIANISM
The main religion of the Persian Empire was Zoroastrianism, which was based on the teachings of the philosopher Zoroaster. It was one of the first religions to be centered on one god, who was believed to be the creator of the world and the source of all goodness. Zoroastrians named their god Ahura Mazda.

Darius I on Persian coin

DARIUS I
Darius I (reigned 522–486 BCE) expanded the Persian Empire to its greatest extent. During his rule, the empire stretched from eastern Europe to the borders of India. The possibility of him conquering Greece ended, however, when he met with defeat at the Battle of Marathon in 490 BCE.

ELITE TROOPS
This colorful mosaic from the royal palace at Susa shows Darius I's elite troops. They were called the Immortals because, according to Greek historians, as soon as one of them was killed he was replaced, maintaining their number always at 10,000. True to its fearsome reputation, the Persian army defeated the Greeks in the Battle of Thermopylae in 480 BCE. Later in 480 BCE, however, Greece won against Persia at the Battle of Salamis. Persia's expansion into Europe was finally brought to an end in 479 BCE with Greece's victory against the Persian army at Plataea.

Tail forms the weight's handle

WEIGHTS AND MEASURES
Lions were symbols of power and royalty in Persia. This bronze lion dating from between the 6th and 4th century BCE was used as a weight for measuring goods. It probably formed part of a set of weights of differing sizes.

Lion weights were common to Middle Eastern civilizations of this time

The Silk Road

THE CIVILIZATIONS OF China and Rome were separated by thousands of miles of deserts and mountains, and at one time the people of each knew nothing of the other culture. News of China reached Europe in the form of silk brought by a long chain of merchants. By the 1st century BCE, a trade network had formed, connecting East with West. Goods such as gold and ivory traveled east, while jade, porcelain, and Chinese silk—the most prized good of all—headed west.

HOW THE SILK ROAD WORKED
The Silk Road worked like a giant relay race, with merchants traveling just as far as they needed to make a trade. There were trading posts along the way. A merchant traveled a short distance to one of these stops, where he sold his cargo of silk, spices, and other goods to another merchant, who then took the trading items farther along the road.

LINKING EAST WITH WEST
In 138 BCE, a Chinese official named Zhang Qian, shown in this mural, was sent by Emperor Wu of the Han Dynasty (p. 29) to try and make an alliance with the people of central Asia. He did not succeed, but the tales he told of the riches that lay to the west encouraged the Chinese to establish a formal trading network.

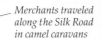

Merchants traveled along the Silk Road in camel caravans

Map of the
Silk Road

FROM ASIA TO EUROPE
Despite its name, the Silk Road was not one single
road. It was a network of trade routes stretching for
more than 4,000 miles (6,400 km). The routes passed
through China, India, Persia, and the Middle East
to reach the West. The map shows one of the most
important routes, direct through central Asia and
Persia. The Silk Road was named after the main item
to be traded along it. Other goods included tea,
ivory, precious stones, and spices.

CHINESE SILK
The cloth that drove the international trade,
silk is a shimmering, luxurious fabric made by weaving
strands from the cocoons of mulberry moths. Developed
in the 4th millennium BCE, the method for making silk
was kept a strict secret by the Chinese for centuries
to keep the price high. Gradually, however, the
secret spread to other countries.

*Roman colonnade at
Palmyra, Syria, which
was an important
caravan stop on
the Silk Road*

PEAK OF THE SILK ROAD
The Silk Road continued from
ancient to medieval times. It
reached its peak in the 13th century
during the Mongol Empire, which
ruled China in 1279–1368. The
Mongols made the Silk Road safer
for merchants to travel and reduced
taxes on the traders, which helped
trade to flourish.

Monument of the Mongolian
emperor, Genghis Khan

THE SPICE ROUTE
The Silk Road was not the first
example of trade between Europe
and Asia. Spices, such as pepper,
cloves, and cinnamon, from India and Indonesia
had been brought to the West by merchants since the
2nd millennium BCE. The spice trade flourished even
more as direct sea links between Europe and China
developed in the 16th century, as the Silk Road declined.

*Coriander
seeds*

*Cinnamon
stick*

Ginger

*Dried rose
petals*

THRACE
MACEDON
AEGEAN SEA
DELPHI
CORINTH • • ATHENS
• SPARTA
CRETE

Ancient Greece
(800–335 BCE)

AFTER THE FALL OF THE MYCENAEAN CIVILIZATION, Greece entered a 400-year "Dark Age," during which its culture declined. A revival began in the eighth century, when villages on the Greek mainland started to join together to form city-states. These city-states shared the same culture, religion, and language, but remained fierce rivals for hundreds of years, often going to war. Eventually, they were conquered and united by the kingdom of Macedon to the north.

SIGNIFICANT CITY-STATES
Most ancient civilizations in Europe and the Middle East were kingdoms or empires in which a large stretch of territory was controlled by a single ruler. Greece, however, was made up of hundreds of independent city-states, each with its own leaders. The largest and most powerful city-states included Athens, Sparta, and Corinth.

ATHENS
Athens was one of the largest and most powerful city-states. It was founded on a hill known as the Acropolis where a large temple, the Parthenon (shown here), was erected during 447–432 BCE. Inside was a huge statue of the city's patron goddess—Athena, the goddess of war.

The long spear was a hoplite's main weapon

The bronze shield was used for protection

WARFARE AND WEAPONS
Greek soldiers, known as hoplites, used long spears as their main weapons. These soldiers were named after the *hoplon*, a large, round shield that was their main protection. When attacking, hoplites lined up in a rectangular formation called a phalanx, with their shields held tightly together and their spears pointing forward.

Hoplites portrayed on a 6th-century BCE vase

Ornate carvings once covered the Parthenon's exterior

Most of the Parthenon is still standing, nearly 2,500 years after it was built

DEMOCRACY

Fed up with unjust rulers, the Athenians invented a new form of government in the 6th century BCE—democracy, which means "people's power." In this system, all free-born Athenian men could vote on the city's laws and decisions at large public gatherings known as "assemblies."

Public voting at an Athenian assembly

Ares, god of war

Crest attached to helmet

THE SPARTANS

No other city-state took warfare as seriously as Sparta. Spartan boys began army life at the age of seven, when they were taken from their families to undergo an intense training system designed to breed tough soldiers. Legendary heroes emerged from among them, such as king Leonidas I, famous for leading the Battle of Thermopylae (480 BCE). Despite the city-state's strict military regime, women in Sparta had much more freedom than in most other Greek cities.

Large shield to protect from thigh to neck

GODS AND GODDESSES

Religion was central to Greek life. The Greeks worshiped many gods, whom they believed lived together on Mount Olympus, Greece's highest mountain. Each god had a responsibility, such as war or the sea, and gods were almost always depicted in human form.

CENTER OF THE WORLD

Delphi was one of the most important religious sites in the Greek world. It had a sanctuary dedicated to the Sun-god, Apollo. At its center stood a stone known as the Omphalos, which the Greeks believed marked the center of the world.

The Omphalos of Delphi

A 1968 statue of Leonidas I at Thermopylae, the site of the famous battle in Greece

Ancient Greek society

THE ANCIENT GREEKS created one of the most influential
societies in history. Their contributions to the fields of science,
philosophy, medicine, and entertainment had a huge effect
on the development of Western civilization. Most Greeks,
however, led simple lives. While men had most of the power and
ran the government, slaves did hard manual labor and
women looked after their homes.

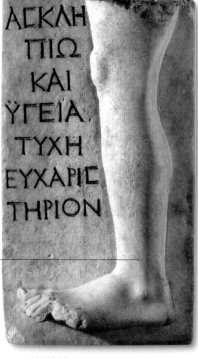

*Greeks sometimes
offered a sculpture of
the body part needing
a cure to Asclepius*

*Plato established
the world's first
philosophy school*

MEDICAL BREAKTHROUGHS
When they became sick, most Greeks
prayed to Asclepius, the god of medicine.
However, the Greek doctor Hippocrates
(c. 460–370 BCE) tried to cure his patients
by observing their symptoms and
prescribing physical treatments. He is
called the "father of modern medicine."

*Aristotle, Plato's pupil,
became Alexander the
Great's tutor*

GREAT THINKERS
Philosophy means "love of wisdom."
It is a way of trying to understand
the world by asking questions. The
Greeks produced several renowned
philosophers, including Socrates
(c. 469–399 BCE), who liked to
explore ideas through discussion. His
pupil Plato (c. 428–348 BCE) founded
a school for philosophers in Athens
known as "The Academy."

Detail from "The
School of Athens,"
a 16th-century
Italian imagining
of ancient
Greek times

DRESSING UP
Men and women didn't dress that differently in ancient Greece. For both, the main item of clothing was the *chiton*, a type of tunic. The Greeks also made jewelry from gold, silver, ivory, and other materials. However, only the rich usually wore jewelry.

Head-shaped gold pendant

Winners were crowned with a wreath of olive leaves

Athletes at the ancient Olympic Games competed without clothes

THE OLYMPIC GAMES
The Greeks staged regular athletic competitions. The most prestigious were the Olympic Games, held every four years in honor of the Greek god Zeus. The games were so important that even wars between the city-states were suspended to allow the competitors to travel freely.

Ancient Greek wine cup in the shape of a ram's head

FOOD AND DRINK
The Greek diet included vegetables and fruits, such as olives, figs, and grapes, that grew on the local mountainous terrain. They also ate bread made from wheat and barley. Meat was usually only served at religious festivals, but cheese and fish were eaten regularly.

Grapes were used to make wine

Copy of an ancient Greek statue showing an Olympic discus thrower

Clay tile roof

All houses had an altar for worship

Small shuttered window

GREEK HOMES
The typical Greek home was made of sun-dried bricks painted white to deflect heat. Larger houses had a central courtyard and perhaps a wooden door—an expensive feature, since wood was scarce in Greece. Often, homes had an entrance porch with a statue of the Greek god Hermes to ward off evil spirits.

Alexander and the Hellenistic age

THOUGH DEFEATED BY THE GREEKS at Plataea in 479 BCE, Persia remained the leading power in the Middle East. The Greeks were busy with their own rivalries and did not focus on extending their territory. But when the Greek city-states were conquered and unified by King Phillip II of Macedon in the mid-4th century BCE, it provided the impetus for Greece to dominate the region like no power had done before. Phillip's son, Alexander, led the Greek armies on a campaign of conquest across the known world.

Alexander battling

ALEXANDER'S EMPIRE
Alexander and his armies arrived in Persia in 334 BCE ready for a fight. Over the next eight years, he fought many battles and conquered the entire Persian Empire and beyond. He claimed territory stretching from Greece and Egypt to India.

THRACE
MACEDON
PHRYGIA
SOGDIANA
SYRIA
BABYLONIA
EGYPT
PERSIA
CARMANIA

Alexander's empire in c. 323 BCE

EARLY LIFE
Alexander's father was King Phillip II of Macedon, a country to the north of Greece. Phillip planned to use the newly unified Greek army to attack the Persian Empire, but died before the campaign could be launched. However, Alexander took over ably. He had not only been trained to be a general, but was also taught to appreciate Greek culture by one of Greece's leading philosophers, Aristotle. Throughout his conquered territories, Alexander promoted Greek culture.

Soldier of Darius III, the defeated Persian king

GREATEST GENERAL
Although just 20 years old when he came to the throne, Alexander went on to prove himself as one of the greatest generals of the ancient world. He never lost a battle, despite often facing forces much larger than his own; this feat led people of his time to regard him as a godlike figure. During his campaigns, he founded 20 cities, all of which he named after himself. The largest, Alexandria in Egypt, would become one of the ancient Mediterranean's leading cities.

Phillip II of Macedon

ALEXANDER'S DEATH

Perhaps the most remarkable thing about Alexander's success was how quickly he achieved it and at what an early age. His great empire was built in 10 years, from 334–323 BCE. Alexander died young, at the age of 32, following a short illness (or possibly poisoning). After his death, his empire was split between his leading generals. This 19th-century painting shows Alexander's soldiers paying tribute to their dying leader.

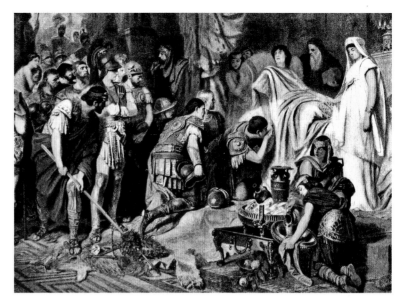

UNITED BY CULTURE

Alexander wanted to build an empire through conquest and cultural influence. He believed that spreading Greek beliefs would unite the conquered people and lessen the chances of his empire disintegrating. He also allowed local leaders to rule their own people, as long as they submitted to his ultimate authority. He felt this would prevent them from rebelling. Even though Alexander's kingdom broke up after his death, the kingdoms that formed continued to mint coins using Alexander's name for the next few centuries.

Gold stater (coin) from the time of Alexander, depicting the goddess Athena

Bucephalus, Alexander's horse

Third-century BCE carving of Alexander leading the fight during his conquest of the Persian Empire

HELLENISTIC STYLE

As Alexander had hoped, Greek culture, traditions, and architectural styles flourished in the territory he conquered after his death, particularly around the Mediterranean. This period became known as the Hellenistic Age after Hellas, the Greek word for Greece. This ruin from the ancient site of Aphrodisias, Turkey, is an example of Hellenistic architecture.

Money

In the early stages of development of most civilizations, people traded by exchanging goods in a system known as barter. Gradually, the idea of using tokens to pay for things became more popular. The value of these tokens—the first kind of money—was agreed upon. From 600 BCE onward, metal coins stamped with a mark—to identify and verify their weight and value—became the standard form of money throughout much of the world. The next major breakthrough was made by the Chinese, who invented banknotes in the 7th century CE.

A source of milk, meat, and work, cattle were considered valuable

BARTERING
Before the invention of money, most trade was done by bartering—swapping one object, such as a cow, for another, such as a bag of grain. Cows were regarded as symbols of wealth in many ancient societies.

Ancient Greek silver coins from the Hellenistic period

Cocoa beans

Chinese knife money

EARLY CURRENCY
People of several ancient civilizations realized that almost anything could be used as currency as long as everyone in the society agreed on its value. The early Chinese used shells to buy goods, the Japanese used rice, while the Maya traded with cocoa beans.

Chinese shovel money

TOOL MONEY
The Chinese began using metal tools, such as shovels and knives, as a form of currency in the 1st millennium BCE. Over time, these became too small and delicate to be used for digging or cutting anything. They changed to symbolic tools, which were used only to buy things.

THE SPREAD OF COINS

Metal coins first appeared around the same time in the mid-1st millennium BCE in China, India, and Lydia (Turkey). Chinese coins had holes, Indian coins were rectangular, while the Lydians produced round coins similar to those used today, with images stamped on the front and back. From Lydia, the use of coins spread to Persia, Greece, Rome, and around the world.

Pile of coins to show the value of the banknote

Image of the Greek emperor was stamped on the coins

CURRENCY TROUBLES

Roman coins were made of gold, silver, bronze, and copper, which made them expensive to produce. Several emperors reduced the amount of precious metal in the coins to save money, which made the coins less valuable. Later emperors tried to solve this problem by making purer coins, such as the *solidus*, a coin used in the Eastern Roman (Byzantine) Empire for around 1,000 years.

Byzantine gold *solidus* depicting Constantine VII, 945 CE

Ming Dynasty banknote from China, 14th century CE

COUNTERFEIT COINS

In Roman times, people made counterfeit (fake) money by covering copper coins with a thin coating of silver or gold. Criminals also stole the metal from coins by cutting away, or "clipping," part of the edge.

BANKNOTES

Early Chinese coins had holes and were carried on strings. As people became richer, the strings got heavier with more and more coins. Then the Chinese began storing their money with friends or colleagues, who gave them IOUs, meaning "I owe you." These were notes saying that one person owed money to another. Later, the IOUs became the first banknotes. The first paper banknotes were created in China in the 7th century CE.

Ancient Rome
(753 BCE–600 CE)

FROM A SMALL CITY-STATE founded in central Italy early in the 1st millennium BCE, Rome grew into a powerful empire stretching across Europe and beyond by 1 CE. In 285 CE, it was split into parts that became the Western and Eastern empires—to make it easier to control. The west, however, was in decline by then and fell to foreign invaders in 476 CE.

ROMAN RULE
Rome was at its peak under the rule of emperor Trajan (reigned 98–117 CE). It controlled territory ranging from Britain in the west to Syria in the east, including much of North Africa. Following the division of the empire, a new capital, Constantinople, was built in the east.

17th-century statue of Julius Caesar in France—he is considered a hero in Western civilization for his military campaigns

ROMULUS AND REMUS
According to Roman legend, Rome was founded by twin brothers, Romulus and Remus, shown in this 14th-century marble work. They were the sons of Mars, the god of war. Abandoned as babies, they were brought up by a wolf. Romulus killed Remus to become Rome's first king, and he named the city after himself.

THE REPUBLIC
Early Rome was ruled by kings. But in 509 BCE, Rome became a Republic, with two rulers (consuls) elected each year to prevent any one person from becoming too powerful. The consuls ruled with the support of the Senate, a parliament of senators—leading aristocrats. Gradually, these aristocrats tried to take control of city wealth, weakening the Republic. In 46 BCE, a leading general, Julius Caesar, seized power for himself, ending the Republic.

END OF THE REPUBLIC

Julius Caesar became Rome's sole leader, or dictator. This angered Rome's politicians, who assassinated him in the Roman Senate in 44 BCE. For the next decade, Rome was plunged into civil war, which was eventually won by Octavian (63 BCE–14 CE), Caesar's adopted son, in 30 BCE.

20th-century painting depicting Julius Caesar's murder

A politician stabbing Caesar in the Senate

THE ROMAN EMPIRE

To secure his position, Octavian pretended to give power back to the Senate but kept the command of the army. He became Rome's first real ruler, taking the name Augustus ("Great One"). His successors took the title *imperator* (commander), which is where the word "emperor" comes from. There was no more power-sharing and Rome became an empire.

Coin from the reign of Augustus

S.P.Q.R.

EXPANSION OF THE EMPIRE

Rome continued to expand its territory during the first two centuries of the empire. Its conquering armies marched behind standards, such as this one bearing the initials S.P.Q.R., which stands for *Senatus Populusque Romanus*, meaning "The Senate and the Roman People." The initials are still used in Rome for official purposes.

Broken sword in the shape of a cross symbolizes Christianity

CONSTANTINE

By the time Constantine (reigned 306–337 CE) came to the throne, Rome was divided into eastern and western halves. He reunited the empire, although later, it split again. He was the first emperor to convert to Christianity, which would eventually become the main religion of the empire. This 20th-century statue of the emperor was erected in York—a city built by the ancient Romans where Constantine had been hailed as emperor.

CONNECTED BY ROADS

The Roman Empire was linked by a great network of stone roads. They were built by the military to allow soldiers to travel quickly so that they could put down uprisings and launch attacks against enemies. But the roads also helped to promote trade, allowing merchants to travel around the empire, selling their goods. Many city streets, such as this one in Pompeii, were also paved with stone.

Life in ancient Rome

THE ROMANS DID NOT RELY ON MILITARY FORCE ALONE to control their empire. They also made deals with local leaders, allowing them to retain control of their regions in return for their support and allowed local people to continue practicing their beliefs. And, perhaps most importantly, they built cities across the empire. Filled with amphitheaters, bathing complexes, and large homes, these cities promoted the Roman way of life, which the locals were encouraged to copy—a process known as "Romanization."

ROMAN CITIES

A lot of what we know about Roman towns comes from the well preserved town of Pompeii, which was buried under ash from the volcanic eruption of Mount Vesuvius. Many people got covered by the ash, which hardened around them. Today, their shapes are preserved, as shown by this plaster cast of a man. Pompeii's town plan was typical of a Roman city. It had a main gate (decuman), a central open space (forum), an amphitheater, and lavish villas.

Amphitheaters were sometimes flooded so reenactments of naval battles could be held

Built in the 1st century CE, the Colosseum still stands today, much of it intact

GAMES AND GLADIATORS

Most Roman cities had an amphitheater—an oval, open-air seated venue where bloodthirsty spectator sports were held, including battles between men and wild animals, and gladiatorial contests where armed warriors fought to the death.

COLOSSEUM

The biggest amphitheater in the Roman world was the Colosseum in Rome, which could hold up to 70,000 spectators. However, the most popular spectator sport in ancient Roman times was probably chariot racing, which took place at special venues called hippodromes.

ROMAN HOUSES

The poor and the rich lived in very different homes. The poor were squeezed together in cramped apartment blocks, while the rich enjoyed much more comfortable conditions. This image shows a cut-away view of a typical townhouse, known as a *domus*, of a well-to-do Roman family. It had large rooms and a courtyard with a pool.

Second-century CE sculpture of Roman pillow seller

Shuttered window

Tiled roof

Courtyard with pool

TRADE AND COMMERCE
Trade routes connected the entire empire by both road and sea, allowing grain, olive oil, craft goods, dyes, fabrics, spices, wine, and other goods to move freely from province to province. The trading was made easier because a single currency was used throughout the empire. Merchants and markets packed the center of every city.

MOSAICS AND FRESCOES
The interiors of the best Roman homes were decorated with fine pieces of art. These included wall paintings called frescoes and pictures (usually laid on the floor) known as mosaics. These mosaics were made by sticking together small clay tiles. Later, mosaics on walls were made with tiny, colored glass pieces. This floor mosaic features a mythical creature called the Medusa, who had snakes for hair and turned anyone who looked at her to stone.

ROMAN BATHS
Bathing in large public baths was a very popular activity across the Roman Empire. The practice itself was a complex process involving a succession of hot and cold pools, steam rooms, and exercise rooms. But bathhouses were also meeting places where people came to socialize. Both men and women enjoyed bathing, although usually they did so at different times of the day.

The well preserved Roman Bath in Bath, England

The Roman army

MUCH OF ROME'S SUCCESS came down to its highly disciplined army. Its soldiers not only conquered an enormous stretch of territory, but also built roads and towns that helped link the empire together. The army was divided into units of around 6,000 men, known as legions. Each was divided into 10 cohorts, which were further divided into groups called centuries. Each century originally had 100 men, but later the number reduced to 80. Military campaigns were led by generals.

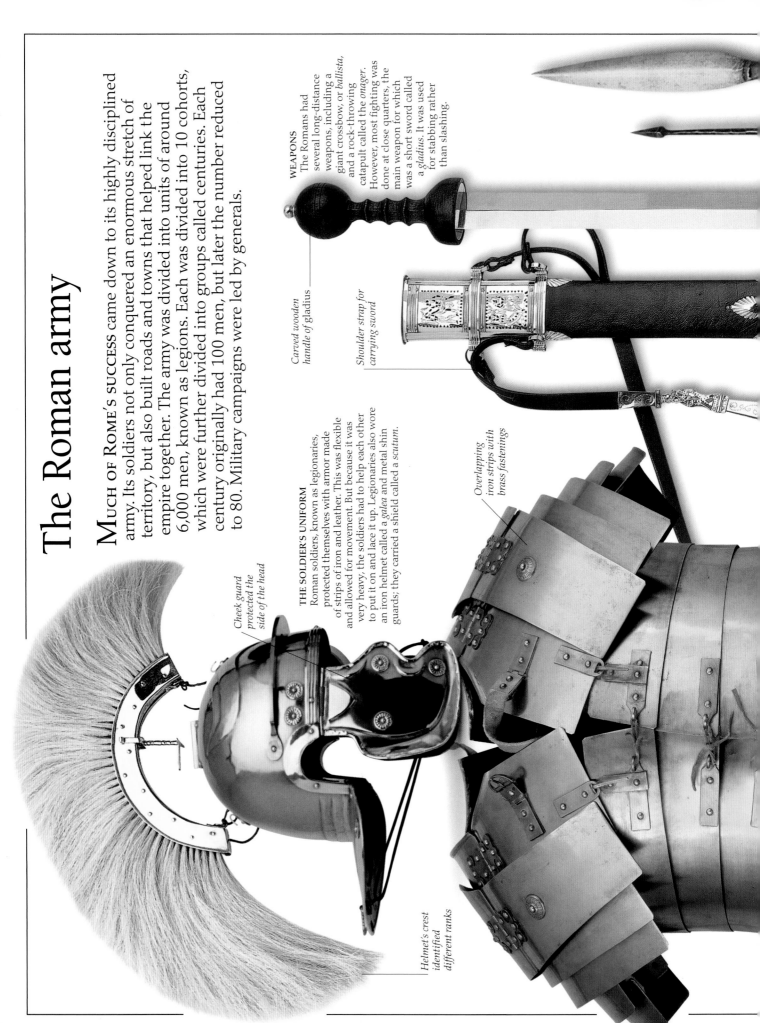

WEAPONS
The Romans had several long-distance weapons, including a giant crossbow, or *ballista*, and a rock-throwing catapult called the *onager*. However, most fighting was done at close quarters, the main weapon for which was a short sword called a *gladius*. It was used for stabbing rather than slashing.

Carved wooden handle of gladius

Shoulder strap for carrying sword

Cheek guard protected the side of the head

THE SOLDIER'S UNIFORM
Roman soldiers, known as legionaries, protected themselves with armor made of strips of iron and leather. This was flexible and allowed for movement. But because it was very heavy, the soldiers had to help each other to put it on and lace it up. Legionaries also wore an iron helmet called a *galea* and metal shin guards; they carried a shield called a *scutum*.

Overlapping iron strips with brass fastenings

Helmet's crest identified different ranks

SPEAR AND JAVELIN

The heavy thrusting spear of the early Roman period (far right) was later replaced by the throwing javelin, or *pilum* (right). A *pilum* was hurled at an opponent from around 65 ft (20 m) away. It was designed to bend on impact so that the enemy could not immediately pick it up and reuse it. After the battle, the Romans gathered the bent javelins and a blacksmith straightened them out again.

Scabbard to sheath sword

Leather sandals (*caligae*) with iron hobnails

Each legion carried a flag called a vexillum

Shields held tightly together

TACTICS AND TORTOISES

If arrows or rocks were being fired at Roman soldiers from above, they adopted the tortoise (*testudo*) formation. This involved holding their shields tightly together, both in front and above them. The shields then acted like the shell of a tortoise to protect them so they couldn't be hit by flying missiles.

Belt with hanging metal straps

Shin guard

Entertainment

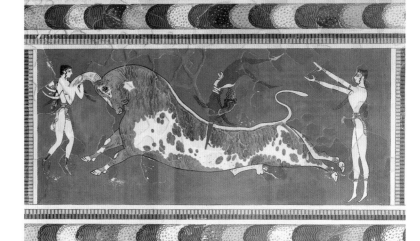

Counter shaped like a jackal

IT IS EASY TO IMAGINE that ancient peoples spent most of their time farming or fighting battles. However, entertainment is not a modern concept—every ancient civilization developed its own forms of entertainment. These ranged from musical performances and theater shows to spectator sports—such as Greece's Olympic Games and Rome's gladiatorial contests. Not only entertaining, these activities often had religious or political significance. Board games and kites also helped to pass the time.

EGYPTIAN GAMES
The Egyptians were particularly fond of board games. Seen above is a hippopotamus-shaped table for playing a game called "dogs and jackals." The goal of this game was to get one's counters all the way around the board before one's opponent.

BULL LEAPING
Frescoes discovered in the palace of Knossos (p. 22) in Minoan Crete (Greece) show male and female athletes doing somersaults over bulls. The image crops up again and again in Minoan art, and some experts suggest that bull leaping was not only a ritual in Minoan society, but also a popular sport.

Game counters

Stick dice

GAMES IN SUMER
This is the oldest board game yet found. Dating from around 2500 BCE, it was discovered in a royal cemetery in the Sumerian city of Ur (pp. 10–11). This inspired its modern name, "The Royal Game of Ur." Players moved counters around a 20-square board by rolling dice. A similar game, Senet, was popular in ancient Egypt.

ATHLETIC COMPETITIONS

Both the ancient Egyptians and the Mesopotamians took part in athletic games, including wrestling and races. The ancient Greeks, however, took these sports to another level, by organizing large inter-city athletic festivals, such as the Olympic Games.

A carving of Greek wrestlers from the 6th century BCE

FLYING KITES

The Chinese invented kites in around 500 BCE. The first models were made of silk and bamboo and were used by the military for signaling. It was only later that kite flying developed as a pastime.

Modern Chinese kite

Teams competed to get a rubber ball through a stone ring such as this one

MAYAN BALL GAME

Ball games were hugely important to the civilizations of Mesoamerica. Almost every Mesoamerican city had a ball court where teams participated in intense matches. Experts believe that these games were played not only for fun but were also part of their rituals.

THEATER

The Greeks loved drama. Almost every Greek town had an open-air theater, some seating up to 15,000 people. The city-states often took part in Greece-wide theatrical competitions. Greece produced many great playwrights whose work is still performed even today. Gradually the Greeks passed on their theatrical traditions to the Romans.

Mask for tragedy

Mask for comedy

Roman mosaic of theatrical masks, from the 2nd century CE

MUSIC

Music was common to all ancient civilizations, most of which developed their own versions of drums, flutes, and stringed instruments. Religious festivals often featured dancing and music. The Moche people (pp. 60–61) of South America made this ceramic trumpet in the 4th century CE.

Playing board is hollow and gaming pieces were stored inside

Mauryan and Gupta India
(321 BCE–550 CE)

IN THE 4TH CENTURY BCE, much of India was controlled by powerful kingdoms called Mahajanapadas. A general named Chandragupta Maurya seized control of the most powerful kingdom, Magadha, and went on a war of conquest, taking over much of India. The new empire grew even larger under emperor Ashoka, who converted to Buddhism and tried to spread it across his kingdom. After his death, the empire broke up into several kingdoms, until the emergence of the Gupta Empire in the 3rd century CE.

MAURYAS AND GUPTAS
This map shows the extent of the Mauryan (in purple) and Gupta (in green) empires. After the collapse of Mauryan power and a period of instability, the Gupta Empire saw a great flourishing of culture, learning, and religion; this period is known as the Golden Age of India.

Chanakya, the emperor's royal adviser

Chandragupta Maurya, who retired in 293 BCE to become a Jain monk

CHANDRAGUPTA MAURYA
Though a very successful general, Chandragupta Maurya was an extremely fearful ruler. He was protected by a bodyguard of 700 women (whom he trusted more than men), never slept in the same bed twice, and had food tasters sample all his meals for poison.

ASHOKA
Ashoka started his reign in 274 BCE as a bloodthirsty, warlike leader. However, in 261 BCE, he fought a brutal campaign in Kalinga, which left him deeply shocked and he decided to convert to Buddhism. He gave up violence and encouraged his subjects to live good lives and to convert to Buddhism. He promoted Buddhism in many ways, such as by building stone structures, which included *stupas*.

END OF MAURYAN RULE

After Ashoka's death, the Mauryan Empire went into decline. The last emperor was killed in 184 BCE, and the empire crumbled. India once again divided into separate states. But Ashoka's reputation grew after his death and he is now regarded as one of India's greatest rulers. His wheel-shaped symbol, called the Ashoka Chakra, features on the modern Indian flag.

Coin showing the lion capital, one of the symbols of Ashoka

The Great Stupa at Sanchi, erected by Ashoka in the 3rd century BCE

THE GUPTA EMPIRE

After centuries of division, India was once again united by the Gupta Dynasty. This began when Chandragupta I came to the throne in Magadha in 320 CE. His successor, Chandragupta II, built the new empire up to its greatest extent, encouraged trade with China and Europe, and became a great patron of the arts. During this period, Hinduism enjoyed the same support as Buddhism did under Ashoka.

A Gupta-period carving of the Hindu god Vishnu on the Dashavatara Temple (c. 500 CE)

THE GOLDEN AGE OF INDIA

Many of the later sacred texts of Hinduism were written during the Gupta period, including the *puranas*, such as the one shown here. This era also saw the emergence of many great Indian scholars, including the playwright Kalidasa. The empire declined in around 550 CE, following an invasion by the Huna people of central Asia.

Moche and Nazca
(100–800 CE)

In AROUND 100 CE, two new civilizations emerged in South America and took the place of the declining Chavín—the Moche of northern Peru and the Nazca of southern Peru. The Moche were the more advanced people, who devised complex irrigation systems, built pyramids, and created elaborate pieces of art. However, the Nazca left their own distinctive legacy in the form of their extraordinary geoglyphs—giant pictures traced on the ground. Both civilizations vanished suddenly in around 800 CE, probably because of changes to the local climate.

MOCHE AND NAZCA TERRITORY
Historians believe that the Moche may have formed South America's first true state. They operated under a single government, rather than a collection of interconnected, but separate, urban units, like the Maya. The Nazca probably never formed a state.

Remains of a warrior

SACRIFICE
Although little is known about Moche religion, it is clear that human sacrifice featured heavily in their rituals. Archeologists have found the remains of sacrificial victims at many Moche sites. Moche art often shows gruesome images of humans being tortured and killed, such as this representation of their "Decapitator God," shown with an ax in one hand and a victim's head in the other.

Human head

Mosaic depicts a Moche warrior

Metalwork model of Moche "Decapitator God" made from flattened gold and copper

ARTS AND CRAFTS
The Moche had a gentler side, too, practicing crafts such as textile weaving and metalworking. They created vast amounts of pottery vessels that looked like representations of animals, people, gods, and many other subjects. Some of them were highly realistic. This earring, made of gold, shells, and colored stones, would have been worn by a Moche ruler.

PYRAMIDS OF THE SUN AND MOON
At the center of the Moche capital were two great step pyramids dedicated to the Sun and the Moon. These structures were the setting for many of the Moche's bloodthirsty rituals. Made of millions of mud bricks, these pyramids were among the largest structures of the ancient Americas.

Large Moche earring

BURIAL

For a people so concerned with death, it is little wonder that Moche burials were elaborate affairs. Moche leaders were buried surrounded by a vast array of goods for use in the afterlife. This image shows the tomb of the Lord of Sipán—a Moche leader—that was discovered intact in 1987, filled with weapons, jewelry, and pottery.

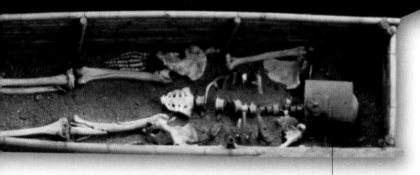

Mummy of the lord wearing a gold and silver necklace

Remains of the standard-bearer

Tomb of the Lord of Sipán

Remains of the lord's wife

Double spout

Stylized picture of a dolphin

THE NAZCA

At the same time as the Moche (100–800 CE), the Nazca culture also thrived on the Peruvian coast. Nazca people built a capital at Cahuachi. These skilled textile weavers and potters often featured images of marine creatures in their art, such as the dolphin on this pot.

NAZCA LINES

The Nazca marked out giant pictures of animals, trees, and flowers, such as this 150-ft- (47-m-) long image of a spider, on the desert ground. It has been preserved by the area's dry, windless climate. These large shapes can only be recognized when we see them from high up in an airplane, so it is likely that the Nazca never fully saw their completed creations. No one knows for sure why these pictures were made, but historians think that the Nazca may have been trying to communicate with their gods.

Greatest cities

ALL GREAT CIVILIZATIONS built great cities. Indeed, the development of large urban centers is one of the defining characteristics of civilizations. Their creation was a sign that a society had advanced to a point where its members could plan, build, and run projects on a large scale. There were many different types of city in the ancient world, from the hilltop states of Athens and Rome to the great coastal trading hub of Alexandria. Whatever their layout or location, cities symbolized the success of a civilization, and their fall was usually the beginning of the end.

URUK
The first great city of the ancient world, Uruk emerged in the world's first urban civilization: Sumer. The *Epic of Gilgamesh* (p. 10) says that the legendary king's tomb was in the bed of Euphrates River in Uruk. Historians believe that the remains shown above could be the tomb mentioned in the epic. Uruk reached its peak in around 2900 BCE, when it may have had 50,000 inhabitants, making it by far the largest city in the world at that time.

A plaza surrounded by many important ancient Roman buildings, the Forum ruins stand at the center of Rome

ROME, THE ETERNAL CITY
Founded on seven hills, Rome was the center of the Roman world, the city on which all other Roman cities were based. But none could rival it for size or grandeur. At its height, ancient Rome was home to more than a million people.

Arch of Septimius Severus, erected by the Roman emperor Septimius Severus

Temple of Saturn

Wild Goose Pagoda, finished in 652 CE during the Tang Dynasty

An artist's impression of the royal hall at Nineveh

XI'AN
One of China's oldest cities, Xi'an became prominent under the Zhou Dynasty (1046–256 BCE). The first Chinese emperor, Qin Shi Huangdi, was buried here in 210 BCE. It became the capital of China in the 3rd century CE and the starting point of the Silk Road (pp. 40–41). By the 9th century CE, it had become the world's largest city.

NINEVEH
Erected as a center of worship for the Mesopotamian goddess Ishtar, Nineveh became the leading city of the Assyrian Empire around 1800 BCE. Here, King Sennacherib ordered the construction of a vast "palace without rival" in around 700 BCE, while his successor, Ashurbanipal, built a vast library containing more than 20,000 cuneiform tablets.

Relief of port of Alexandria on terra-cotta oil lamp

ALEXANDRIA
Founded on the Egyptian coast by Alexander the Great around 331 BCE, Alexandria grew to become one of the Mediterranean's largest cities. It was the site of a famous library and an enormous lighthouse, which was regarded as one of the Seven Wonders of the Ancient World.

Female figures on the porch

ATHENS
One of the great city-states of ancient Greece, Athens was founded on a hill known as the Acropolis. As the city grew, new sections were added to the lower slopes, while the hilltop became the city's most sacred place and the site of the Parthenon temple. Here we see the Erechtheion temple at the Acropolis.

Timeline

THE GREAT CIVILIZATIONS of the past developed at different times and at different rates. Here you can see their rise, from the first farmers to the building of mighty cities, as well as their fall, as each in turn either faded away or was toppled by newer, more powerful rivals.

Tracing ancient footsteps

Take a walk through time to discover some of the important milestones of human history in ancient times.

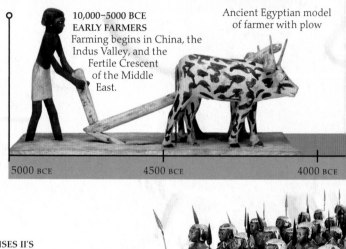

10,000–5000 BCE EARLY FARMERS
Farming begins in China, the Indus Valley, and the Fertile Crescent of the Middle East.

Ancient Egyptian model of farmer with plow

5000 BCE	4500 BCE	4000 BCE

Breastplate of Ramses II

1279 BCE RAMSES II'S REIGN BEGINS
Ramses II becomes the pharaoh of Egypt's New Kingdom and goes on to rule until 1213 BCE.

Model of Nubian soldiers from ancient Egypt

1400 BCE	1300 BCE	1200 BCE	1100 BCE	1000 BCE

1400 BCE MYCENAEAN CIVILIZATION
The Mycenaeans take over the Minoan civilization and gain control of the island of Crete.

1200 BCE TRADE NETWORK
The Phoenicians begin to establish a trading network across the Mediterranean from their home in the Levant region.

Phoenician glass beads, an important trade item

900 BCE CHAVÍN CULTURE EMERGES
In South America, the Chavín civilization begins to rise in Peru and becomes an important culture in the region.

Chavín pottery

30 BCE AUGUSTUS COMES TO THE THRONE
The Roman Empire is founded by Augustus, and Egypt becomes a province of the Roman Empire.

30 BCE	100 CE	200 CE	300 CE	400 CE

100 CE MOCHE CULTURE EMERGES
In South America, the Moche culture begins to flourish in northern Peru, forming the region's first true state.

Moche ceramic jar

Diocletian on ancient Roman coin

285 CE ROMAN EMPIRE IS DIVIDED
The weakening Roman Empire is divided by Emperor Diocletian and develops into Western and Eastern empires.

400 CE NAZCA LINES ARE DRAWN
In South America, the first Nazca lines—giant pictures drawn on the ground—are created in southern Peru.

Nazca lines

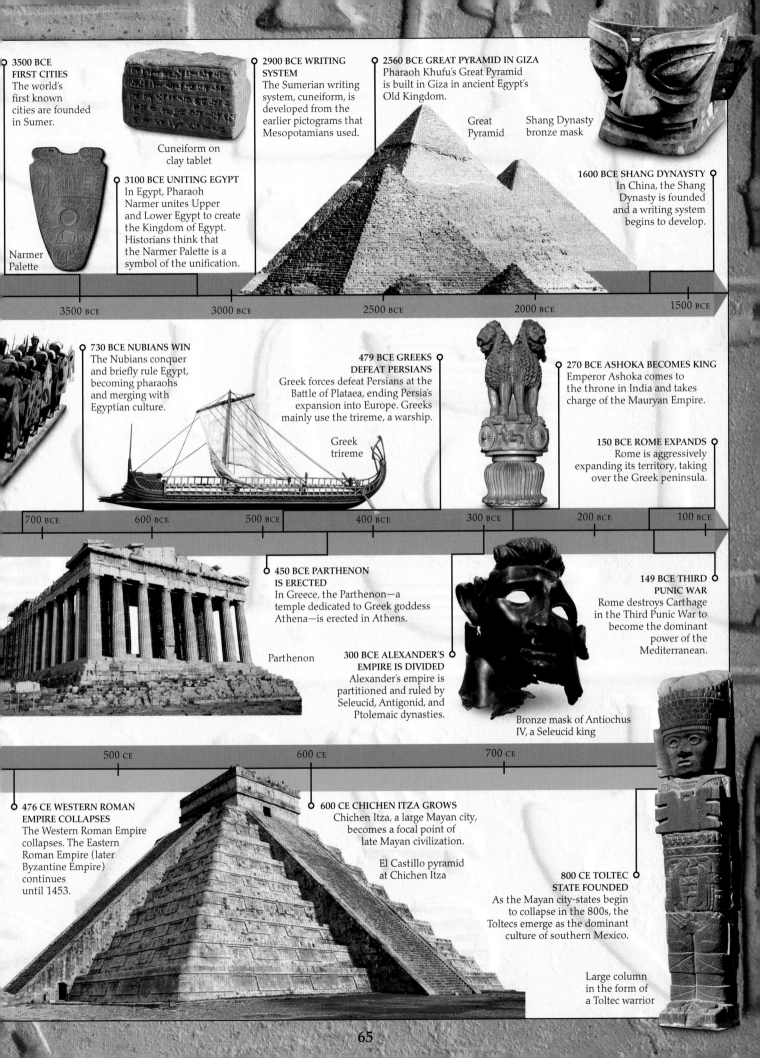

3500 BCE
FIRST CITIES
The world's first known cities are founded in Sumer.

Cuneiform on clay tablet

Narmer Palette

3100 BCE UNITING EGYPT
In Egypt, Pharaoh Narmer unites Upper and Lower Egypt to create the Kingdom of Egypt. Historians think that the Narmer Palette is a symbol of the unification.

2900 BCE WRITING SYSTEM
The Sumerian writing system, cuneiform, is developed from the earlier pictograms that Mesopotamians used.

2560 BCE GREAT PYRAMID IN GIZA
Pharaoh Khufu's Great Pyramid is built in Giza in ancient Egypt's Old Kingdom.

Great Pyramid

Shang Dynasty bronze mask

1600 BCE SHANG DYNAYSTY
In China, the Shang Dynasty is founded and a writing system begins to develop.

3500 BCE   3000 BCE   2500 BCE   2000 BCE   1500 BCE

730 BCE NUBIANS WIN
The Nubians conquer and briefly rule Egypt, becoming pharaohs and merging with Egyptian culture.

Greek trireme

479 BCE GREEKS DEFEAT PERSIANS
Greek forces defeat Persians at the Battle of Plataea, ending Persia's expansion into Europe. Greeks mainly use the trireme, a warship.

270 BCE ASHOKA BECOMES KING
Emperor Ashoka comes to the throne in India and takes charge of the Mauryan Empire.

150 BCE ROME EXPANDS
Rome is aggressively expanding its territory, taking over the Greek peninsula.

700 BCE   600 BCE   500 BCE   400 BCE   300 BCE   200 BCE   100 BCE

450 BCE PARTHENON IS ERECTED
In Greece, the Parthenon—a temple dedicated to Greek goddess Athena—is erected in Athens.

Parthenon

300 BCE ALEXANDER'S EMPIRE IS DIVIDED
Alexander's empire is partitioned and ruled by Seleucid, Antigonid, and Ptolemaic dynasties.

Bronze mask of Antiochus IV, a Seleucid king

149 BCE THIRD PUNIC WAR
Rome destroys Carthage in the Third Punic War to become the dominant power of the Mediterranean.

500 CE   600 CE   700 CE

476 CE WESTERN ROMAN EMPIRE COLLAPSES
The Western Roman Empire collapses. The Eastern Roman Empire (later Byzantine Empire) continues until 1453.

600 CE CHICHEN ITZA GROWS
Chichen Itza, a large Mayan city, becomes a focal point of late Mayan civilization.

El Castillo pyramid at Chichen Itza

800 CE TOLTEC STATE FOUNDED
As the Mayan city-states begin to collapse in the 800s, the Toltecs emerge as the dominant culture of southern Mexico.

Large column in the form of a Toltec warrior

Ancient innovations

A NUMBER OF KEY INVENTIONS and technological advances helped civilizations to progress, build their own societies, and explore other societies and cultures that were far away from them. The ancient world developed many things that are still in use, with some additions and refinements. Here are some of the greatest leaps made by ancient civilizations.

Pottery

Every civilization produces surpluses of food that have to be stored. Experts feel that pottery was invented as a way of storing this extra food. Some of the earliest pots were created in 13,000 BCE by the Jomon people of ancient Japan.

Early Jomon earthenware

Crops and farm animals

Agriculture was the invention that kick-started civilization, allowing people to settle down and build permanent villages. Farming began in an area of the Middle East known as the Fertile Crescent around 10,000 years ago.

Barley, one of the earliest crops grown

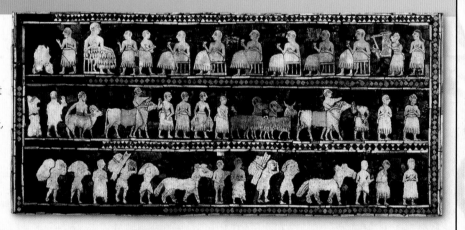

Images of farming, Mesopotamia, 2600 BCE

Metal tools and weapons

The earliest human tools were made of wood, bones, and stone. As people learned to extract metal from ore, they could make harder, sharper tools and weapons. The earliest metal weapons, found in Serbia, were made from copper and date from around 5500 BCE.

Bronze socketed spearhead, Luristan, Iran (c. 1000–800 BCE)

Bronze ax blade with a curved edge (c. 950–750 BCE)

Bronze Age ax blades (c. 1500 BCE)

Shang Dynasty (1600–1027 BCE) bronze ax

The boat

Although there is no solid proof, historians think that the first people to reach Australia did so by sea, probably in simple log boats, at a time when the crossing was shorter than it is now. The oldest boats yet discovered are the oar boats that sailed on the Nile River around 7500–7000 BCE. The next breakthrough was the invention of sails in Sumeria around 6,000 years ago. With life centered on the Nile River, Egyptians used boats for fishing, transporting goods, and as royal and funeral barges.

Ancient Egyptian model of a boat carrying a mummy to its tomb

Canopy

Mourner

Curved end piece

The wheel

The invention of the wheel set the modern world turning. The earliest wheel comes from Mesopotamia around 3500 BCE, although it was a potter's wheel and would not be adapted for use on vehicles for a few hundred years. The image shows ancient Chinese wooden chariots recovered from a Zhou Dynasty (1027–481 BCE) tomb in Luoyang.

Writing

Different civilizations invented various writing systems and tools that allowed them to write down their beliefs and record their history. In the 3rd millennium BCE, Egyptians became the first to use a paperlike writing surface made from strips of papyrus reed.

Egyptian contract in demotic script on a papyrus sheet (553 BCE)

Greatest rulers

CIVILIZATIONS ARE BUILT by many people working together toward a common goal. Yet their efforts would be for nothing without great leadership. The most successful rulers of the ancient world were usually excellent military commanders, conquering huge empires and ruling many people. But the best also supported the growth of culture, encouraging learning, science, and the arts. These pages compare and contrast some of the ancient world's most celebrated rulers—those who had the greatest influence on their period of history.

SARGON OF AKKAD

The first emperor

- **RULER OF**   Akkadian Empire
- **REIGN**   c. 2270–2215 BCE
- **FAMOUS FOR** Sargon conquered Mesopotamian city-states to create the world's first empire, which stretched from the Persian Gulf to the Mediterranean.

TAHARQA

Ruler of two kingdoms

- **RULER OF**   Nubia and Egypt
- **REIGN**   c. 690–664 BCE
- **FAMOUS FOR** Following the conquest of Egypt by Nubia, Pharaoh Taharqa oversaw a period of prosperity for the two kingdoms.

ASHURBANIPAL

The great librarian

- **RULER OF**   Assyrian Empire
- **REIGN**   668–627 BCE
- **FAMOUS FOR** In addition to being a fierce warrior, Ashurbanipal was also a great promoter of learning, building a huge library at his capital, Nineveh.

NEBUCHADNEZZAR II

King of gardening

- **RULER OF**   Babylonian Empire
- **REIGN**   c. 605–562 BCE
- **FAMOUS FOR** Nebuchadnezzar turned Babylon into the Middle East's finest city, famed for its mighty gates and luxurious hanging gardens.

ASHOKA

The serene warrior

- **RULER OF**   Mauryan Empire
- **REIGN**   274–232 BCE
- **FAMOUS FOR** Although he fought many battles, Ashoka is more famed for giving up war and promoting morality after he adopted Buddhism as his religion.

QIN SHI HUANGDI

Terra-cotta warrior

- **RULER OF**   China
- **REIGN**   221–210 BCE
- **FAMOUS FOR** The first emperor of China, Qin Shi Huangdi was buried alongside a great army of more than 8,000 clay soldiers.

AUGUSTUS

The founding father

- **RULER OF**   Roman Empire
- **REIGN**   27 BCE–14 CE
- **FAMOUS FOR** Augustus was the first emperor of Rome. He put an end to years of civil war, bringing peace to Rome.

HATSHEPSUT

The female pharaoh

- **RULER OF** Egypt
- **REIGN** c. 1479–1458 BCE
- **FAMOUS FOR** One of the few female rulers of ancient Egypt, Hatshepsut enjoyed a successful reign, building up trading links with other civilizations.

TUTHMOSIS III

Pharaoh power

- **RULER OF** Egypt
- **REIGN** 1479–1425 BCE
- **FAMOUS FOR** Initially sharing power with his stepmother Hatshepsut, Tuthmosis extended Egypt's borders as far as they would ever reach.

RAMSES II

The shameless self-promoter

- **RULER OF** Egypt
- **REIGN** 1279–1213 BCE
- **FAMOUS FOR** Regarded as one of Egypt's greatest pharaohs—not least by himself—Ramses had many monuments and temples erected in his own honor.

CYRUS THE GREAT

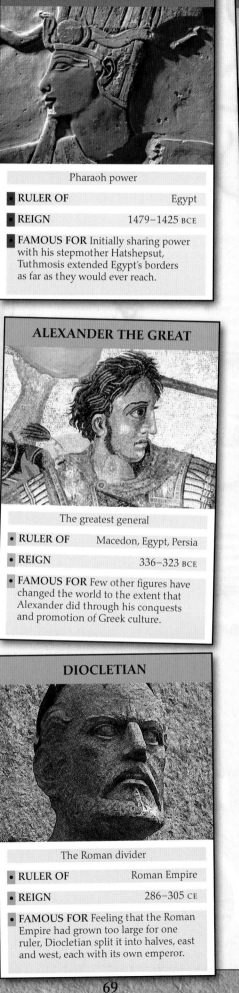

Fast and furious

- **RULER OF** Persian Empire
- **REIGN** 559–530 BCE
- **FAMOUS FOR** No previous ruler in the Middle East had been as successful as quickly as Cyrus, who conquered all the region's major empires.

ALEXANDER THE GREAT

The greatest general

- **RULER OF** Macedon, Egypt, Persia
- **REIGN** 336–323 BCE
- **FAMOUS FOR** Few other figures have changed the world to the extent that Alexander did through his conquests and promotion of Greek culture.

CHANDRAGUPTA MAURYA

First unifier of India

- **RULER OF** Mauryan Empire
- **REIGN** 320–298 BCE
- **FAMOUS FOR** Chandragupta founded the Mauryan Empire and was the first Indian ruler to unify such a large territory in the Indian subcontinent.

TRAJAN

The great rebuilder

- **RULER OF** Roman Empire
- **REIGN** 98–117 CE
- **FAMOUS FOR** Under Trajan, the Roman Empire reached its greatest extent while Rome enjoyed a massive rebuilding program.

DIOCLETIAN

The Roman divider

- **RULER OF** Roman Empire
- **REIGN** 286–305 CE
- **FAMOUS FOR** Feeling that the Roman Empire had grown too large for one ruler, Diocletian split it into halves, east and west, each with its own emperor.

CONSTANTINE THE GREAT

The imperial converter

- **RULER OF** Roman Empire
- **REIGN** 306–337 CE
- **FAMOUS FOR** Constantine fought numerous battles to unify the empire divided by Diocletian and became the first emperor to convert to Christianity.

Glossary

AGRICULTURE
The planting and harvesting of crops, and the rearing of animals. Also known as farming.

ARCHEOLOGY
Learning about past civilizations through discovering and uncovering their physical remains—the buildings, objects, and records that the people left behind.

ASSASSINATE
To kill a ruler or any other political figure.

BCE
Used to describe the period before the year 1 CE. It stands for "Before Common Era."

BOG
A wetland where deposits of plant material, called peat, build up. The lack of oxygen in peat bogs preserves archeological remains for centuries.

BRONZE AGE
A period of ancient history when civilizations made weapons and tools from bronze, an alloy (mixture) of copper and tin. Bronze ages took place at different times in different civilizations, but usually after the Stone Age and before the Iron Age.

BUDDHISM
A religion based on the teachings of Siddhartha Gautama, later known as the Buddha, who lived in India in the 5th century BCE.

Statue of the Buddha

CAMPAIGN
A series of battles fought to achieve a military objective.

CARAVAN
A train of animals, usually camels, linked together and used to transport goods across long distances. Camel caravans were often used on the Silk Road.

CE
Used to describe the period after 1 CE, the year of Jesus' birth. It stands for "Common Era."

CHRISTIANITY
A religion based on the teachings of Jesus, who lived in the Roman province of Judea in the 1st century CE.

CITY-STATE
A city that is ruled by an independent government.

CIVIL WAR
A war between two groups within a state or region that had previously been united.

CIVILIZATION
A society whose people farm, live in towns and cities, produce food in plenty, employ people in many different jobs, have a social hierarchy, and are ruled by a government.

COUNTERFEIT
A fake version of a real object, such as a coin or a work of art.

CUNEIFORM
A writing system developed by the Sumerians in 2900 BCE. It was written by making marks in wet pieces of clay using a reed.

CURRENCY
Tokens, or money, used within a society to purchase goods.

DEMOCRACY
A system of government developed in ancient Athens whereby laws were voted upon by all freeborn men over the age of 20.

DEMOTIC
A system of writing developed in ancient Egypt for everyday use as a simpler, quicker alternative to hieroglyphics.

DICTATOR
A supreme leader appointed in ancient Rome for a period of just six months to deal with a crisis. Julius Caesar started a civil war by declaring himself "dictator for life."

Coin showing Julius Caesar, a dictator

DYNASTY
A family that retains power for several generations, with each leader drawn from the same family.

EMPEROR
The sole ruler of an empire.

EMPIRE
A number of previously separate states or regions that are brought under the control of a single ruler or authority, usually by conquest.

FERTILE CRESCENT
A crescent-shaped region in the Middle East where it is believed farming first began around 8000 BCE.

FLOODPLAINS
The areas on each side of a river onto which the river frequently floods. These areas often have very fertile soil, which is why many early civilizations developed on floodplains.

GOVERNMENT
The body that rules, or governs, a state, empire, or country.

HELLENISTIC
Describes societies or cultures that were influenced by the ancient Greek civilization, particularly after the conquests of Alexander in the 4th century BCE.

HEREDITARY
Passed from one generation to the next.

HIERARCHY
The division of society into groups, or classes, according to their wealth and power. A typical hierarchy from the ancient world would have the king at the top and slaves at the bottom.

HIEROGLYPHICS
A form of ancient Egyptian writing. It means "sacred writing."

Senate, a part of the Roman Republic

HINDUISM
An Indian religion based on a wide range of teachings and writings built up over time, beginning in the 2nd millennium BCE.

INNOVATION
A new invention, process, or way of doing things.

IRON AGE
A period of ancient history when civilizations made weapons and tools from iron. Iron ages started at different times in different civilizations, but usually after the Bronze Age.

IRRIGATION
Getting water to flow from a water source, such as a river, to an area of dry land, such as a field.

IVORY
A material from the tusks of animals (usually elephants), often used for carving.

JADE
A naturally occurring green stone that was highly prized in China and Mesoamerican civilizations.

Ancient Egyptian headrest made from ivory

JAINISM
A religion founded in India in the 1st millennium BCE that preaches nonviolence toward all living things.

MESOAMERICA
A region now occupied by central and southern Mexico, Belize, Guatemala, Nicaragua, El Salvador, and Honduras where many ancient civilizations, including the Maya, arose.

MESOPOTAMIA
A region of the Middle East between the Tigris and Euphrates rivers where the world's first civilization of Sumer was founded.

MONARCHY
A form of government in which the people are ruled by a king (or queen), who is usually part of a dynasty.

MUMMY
A dead body that has been preserved.

MYTHS
Stories told about the creation and early history of a civilization, often featuring gods and monsters.

OLYMPIC GAMES (ANCIENT)
An athletic competition and religious festival held in Greece every four years between 776 BCE and 394 CE.

ORNATE
Featuring complex patterns or decorations.

PAPYRUS
A type of reed that grows by the Nile River and was used by the Egyptians to make a wide range of objects, including paper, baskets, rope, and boats.

PHARAOH
The head of state in ancient Egypt—the equivalent of a king. It means "great house," a reference to the royal palace.

PHILOSOPHY
A way of thinking about the world, how it works, and how people behave. It means "love of wisdom" in Greek.

PLAZA
An open space in a city, such as a square.

PORCH
A covered entrance to a building.

PYRAMID
A type of building with four sides, a wide bottom, and a narrow top, erected by several ancient civilizations, including the Egyptians and the Maya.

REED
A grasslike plant, the stems of which were used to make writing implements in Sumer and ancient Egypt.

REPUBLIC
A type of government in ancient Rome designed to stop any one individual from becoming too powerful. Under the Republic, Rome was governed by two elected leaders, called consuls, who were allowed to rule for just one year. Today, a republic is any state that is not ruled by a monarch.

RITUAL
A series of activities usually performed as part of a religious ceremony.

SACRIFICE
To kill something (or someone) or to give up something precious (such as food or weapons) in honor of a god (or gods).

Ritual involving a Mayan king

SCARAB
A type of beetle that was often featured in ancient Egyptian art and jewelry. The Egyptians believed a beetle rolled the Sun across the sky each day.

SEAL
A device for making a mark on a piece of clay or wax to indicate ownership of something.

SEVEN WONDERS OF THE ANCIENT WORLD
A list of the ancient world's most impressive structures, as compiled in the 2nd century BCE by Greek historians. They were the Hanging Gardens of Babylon; the Mausoleum of Halikarnassus; the Temple of Artemis at Ephesus; the Lighthouse at Alexandria; the Colossus of Rhodes; the Statue of Zeus at Olympia; and the Great Pyramid of Giza.

SILK ROAD
A 4,000-mile- (6,400-km-) long overland trade route that linked China in the east with the Mediterranean region in the west. It was named after Chinese silk, one of the most precious trading commodities.

SOCIETY
A group of people that shares the same culture and beliefs, and often the same government.

STATE
A society or region ruled by a single government.

STYLUS
A writing tool made from a cut reed used for making impressions in wax or clay.

TERRA-COTTA
A type of ceramic made from clay.

URBAN
Describes an area such as a city or town where many people live together in close-set buildings.

Index

Acknowledgments

Dorling Kindersley would like to thank:
Helen Peters for the index, Stewart Wild for proofreading, and Kingshuk Ghoshal for editorial assistance.

The publisher would like to thank the following for their kind permission to reproduce their photographs:

(Key: a-above; b-below/bottom; c-center; f-far; l-left; r-right; t-top)

1 **Corbis**: (c). 2 **Alamy Images**: Gianni Dagli Orti / The Art Archive (tc, cr). **Corbis**: Gianni Dagli Orti (ca). **Getty Images**: DEA / A. Dagli Orti (tl); Raphael / The Bridgeman Art Library (bl). 2-3 **Getty Images**: De Agostini (bc). 3 **Alamy Images**: Ron Nickel / Design Pics Inc. (tl/coins). **Dorling Kindersley**: Egyptian Museum, Cairo (c). **Dreamstime.com**: Gavran333 (tl). 4 **Alamy Images**: Ancient Art & Architecture Collection Ltd (cra). **The Bridgeman Art Library**: Zev Radovan (tr). **Corbis**: Heritage Images (crb); Sandro Vannini (br). **Dorling Kindersley**: Ermine Street Guard (t, tl). **Getty Images**: DEA / G. Nimatallah (cla); DEA / G. Dagli Orti (bl). 5 **Getty Images**: DEA / G. Dagli Orti (tr). 6 **Corbis**: Sandro Vannini (c). **Getty Images**: Oliviero Olivieri / Robert Harding World Imagery (t). 6-7 **Getty Images**: Herbert M. Herget / National Geographic Society (b). 7 **Corbis**: Gianni Dagli Orti (tr); Mimmo Jodice (tl); Daniel LeClair / Reuters (cr); Heritage Images (br). 8 **Dorling Kindersley**: Natural History Museum, London (bl). **Dreamstime.com**: Mquirk (fcl). **Rex Features**: Peter Brooker (cl). 8-9 **Corbis**: Mockford & Bonetti / Eye Ubiquitous (c). 9 **Corbis**: Supreme Council for Antiquities / Handout / Reuters (cr). **Getty Images**: Time Life Pictures (cr). **Science Photo Library**: James King-Holmes (tl). 10 **Getty Images**: DEA / G. Dagli Orti (tl). **SuperStock**: Science and Society (cb). 10-11 **Alamy Images**: Zuma Wire Service (b). 11 **Alamy Images**: Ancient Art & Architecture Collection Ltd (t). **Corbis**: Gianni Dagli Orti (cl). **Getty Images**: DEA / A. De Gregorio (cr). 12-13 **Corbis**: Bernard Annebicque / Sygma (cra). 12 **Corbis**: Sandro Vannini (cra). 13 **Corbis**: Jose Fuste Raga (tl); Sandro Vannini (tr). **Getty Images**: Dea Picture Library / Egyptian / The Bridgeman Art Library (c). 14-15 **Getty Images**: Dea / A. Jemolo (br). 14 **Corbis**: Gianni Dagli Orti (cra). **Photoshot**: DeAgostini \UIG (tl). 15 **Dorling Kindersley**: The Trustees of the British Museum (tr, tr/Situla). **Getty Images**: Danita Delimont / Gallo Images (cr); DEA / G. Dagli Orti (bl). 16 **Getty Images**: De Agostini Pict.Lib. (tl). **Alamy Images**: Ancient Art & Architecture Collection Ltd (c). **Corbis**: Gianni Dagli Orti (bl). 16-17 **Dorling Kindersley**: Egyptian

Museum, Cairo (c). 17 **Getty Images**: Egyptian 18th Dynasty / The Bridgeman Art Library (br). 18 **Alamy Images**: Angelo Hornak (cr). 18-19 **Getty Images**: James L. Stanfield / National Geographic (b). 19 **Alamy Images**: Angelo Hornak (c). **Corbis**: (cra); Angelo Hornak (tl, cl); Luca Tettoni (br). **Getty Images**: Harappan / The Bridgeman Art Library (tc). 20 **Corbis**: Gianni Dagli Orti (b). **Getty Images**: Dea / E. Lessing (cr); DEA / V. Pirozzi (tl). 21 **Alamy Images**: Angelo Hornak (c). **Corbis**: Robert Harding Picture Library Ltd (cl). **Corbis**: Chris Warren / LOOP IMAGES / Loop Images (tl). **Getty Images**: Werner Forman / Universal Images Group (r). 22 **Getty Images**: De Agostini (cr, br); DEA / G. Dagli Orti (bl). 23 **Alamy Images**: Gianni Dagli Orti / The Art Archive (tr). **Corbis**: Fridmar Damm (c). **Getty Images**: Universal ImagesGroup (bl). 24 **Alamy Images**: Prisma Archivo (bl). 24-25 **Getty Images**: DEA / A. Jemolo (c). 25 **Alamy Images**: INTERFOTO (br). **Getty Images**: Herbert M. Herget / National Geographic Society (t). **SuperStock**: Image Asset Management Ltd. (cr). 26 **Alamy Images**: Gianni Dagli Orti / The Art Archive (c); Peter Horree (bl). 26-27 **Corbis**: Danny Lehman (c). 27 **Corbis**: Heritage Images; Werner Forman (c). **Getty Images**: Olmec / The Bridgeman Art Library (tr). 28-29 **Dreamstime.com**: Hungchungchih (b). 28 **Corbis**: Burstein Collection (c). **Dreamstime.com**: Tomboy2290 (cra). 29 **Alamy Images**: The Art Archive (tl). **Corbis**: Asian Art & Archaeology, Inc. (cra). **Getty Images**: Chinese School / The Bridgeman Art Library (tc). 30 **Dorling Kindersley**: The Trustees of the British Museum (bc). **Getty Images**: Dea / S. Vannini (b); Science & Society Picture Library (t). 30-31 **Dorling Kindersley**: The Trustees of the British Museum (bc). 31 **Corbis**: Brooklyn Museum (cr). **Getty Images**: DEA / G. Nimatallah (tl, br); Dea Picture Library / De Agostini Picture Library (bc). 32 **Getty Images**: Francois Guillot / AFP (tl). 32-33 **Getty Images**: Science & Society Picture Library (bc). 33 **Corbis**: (tr); Mohamed Messara / Epa (c). **Dreamstime.com**: Olga Yastremska (tl). **Getty Images**: DEA / A. Dagli Orti (br). 34 **Getty Images**: Dea Picture Library / De Agostini Picture Library (bl). 34-35 **Alamy Images**: Gianni Dagli Orti / The Art Archive (c). 35 **Dreamstime.com**: Tomasz Pado (tl). **Getty Images**: Aztec / The Bridgeman Art Library (c). 36 **Corbis**: The Gallery Collection (tl). **Getty Images**: Mesopotamian / The Bridgeman Art Library (c). 36-37 **Alamy Images**: Zev Radovan / www. BibleLandPictures.com (b). 37 **Getty Images**: Atta Kenare / AFP (cr). 38-39 **Getty Images**: Dea Picture Library / De Agostini Picture Library (tc). **Panos Pictures**: Marcus Rose (b). 39

41 **Corbis**: Paul Schiefer Photography / the food passionates (tr). **Getty Images**: Massimo Pizzotti / Photographer's Choice (c). 42 **akg-images**: De Agostini Pict.Lib. (c). **Dreamstime.com**: Natalia Pavlova (b). 43 **Alamy Images**: Constantinos Iliopoulos (bl). **Getty Images**: Mimmo Jodice (cl); Herbert M. Herget / National Geographic Society (tc). 44 **akg-images**: Erich Lessing / British Museum (tr). **Getty Images**: Raphael / The Bridgeman Art Library (b). 45 **Alamy Images**: RM Images (cr). **Dorling Kindersley**: Bill Gordon - modelmaker (c). **Getty Images**: DEA / G. Dagli Orti (tl); DEA / G. Nimatallah (cr). 46 **Getty Images**: DEA / G. Dagli Orti (bl). 46-47 **Getty Images**: DEA / G. Dagli Orti (bc). 47 **Alamy Images**: North Wind Picture Archives (tr); Prisma / Raga Jose Fuste / Prisma Bildagentur AG (br). **Corbis**: Hoberman Collection (cr). 48-49 **Dreamstime.com**: Gavran333 (c). 48 **Alamy Images**: Ron Nickel / Design Pics Inc. (c); Panorama Media (Beijing) Ltd. (bc, br). **Dreamstime.com**: Foodmaniac (bl). 49 **Corbis**: Hoberman Collection (tr); Werner Forman (cl). **Dorling Kindersley**: The Trustees of the British Museum (bl). **Mary Evans Picture Library**: Iberfoto (c). 50 **Alamy Images**: Peter Horree (l). **Corbis**: Fred de Noyelle / Godong (crb). **Getty Images**: Ivy Close Images (cl). **Corbis**: Arctic-Images (clb). **Dorling Kindersley**: The Trustees of the British Museum (r). **Getty Images**: Ken Scicluna / AWL Images (tr). **Photoshot**: Peter Brown (br). 52-53 **Getty Images**: Hoberman Collection / Universal Images Group (b). 52 **Corbis**: Michael Nicholson (cra). 53 **Corbis**: Tetra Images (tr). **Getty Images**: DEA / G. Nimatallah (cla); **SuperStock** (t). 54-55 **Dorling Kindersley**: University Museum of Newcastle (bc). 54 **Dorling Kindersley**: Ermine Street Guard (cb, cra, bl). 55 **Dorling Kindersley**: Ermine Street Guard (t, cla); University Museum of Newcastle (cr, br). **Dreamstime.com**: Regien Paassen (cra). 56 **Alamy Images**: Gianni Dagli Orti / The Art Archive (tr). **Getty Images**: Zev Radovan / www.BibleLandPictures.com (b). 57 **Dreamstime.com**: Jinfeng Zhang (tr). **Getty Images**: De Agostini Picture Library (cra); DEA / G. Dagli Orti (cl, br); DEA / G. Nimatallah (cl). 58 **The Bridgeman Art Library**: Dinodia (clb). 58-59 **SuperStock**: De Agostini (bc). 59 **The Bridgeman Art Library**: Giraudon (t). **Corbis**: Thom Lang (tc). **Getty Images**: British Library / Robana / Hulton Fine Art Collection (c). 60 **Alamy Images**: Nathan Benn (c). **Corbis**: Gianni Dagli Orti (bl). 60-61 **Alamy Images**: Reciprocity Images (b). 61 **Getty Images**: Kevin Schafer (c). 61 **Getty Images**: Danita Delimont / Gallo Images (clb); DEA / G. Dagli Orti (b). 62 **Getty Images**: Essam Al-Sudani / AFP (tr). 62-63 **Getty Images**: Zens photo / Flickr (b). 63 **Corbis**: Tuul / Hemis (br); PoodlesRock (tr). **Getty Images**: Dea Picture Library / De Agostini Picture Library (tl); Chu Yong (tl). 64 **Alamy Images**: Prisma Archivo (crb). **Corbis**: David Lees (cb); Werner Forman (bl).

Dorling Kindersley: The Trustees of the British Museum (tl). 64-65 **Corbis**: Ron Watts (Background). 65 **Getty Images**: Egyptian 19th Dynasty / The Bridgeman Art Library (cl); Roman / The Bridgeman Art Library (bc); Danita Delimont / Gallo Images (br); Jürgen Liepe (bc). 64-65 **Corbis**: Ron Watts (Background). Indian, (3rd century BC) / The Art Gallery Collection (cra); Gianni Dagli Orti / The Art Archive (crb). **Corbis**: Asian Art & Archaeology, Inc. (tr); Sandro Vannini (tl/Narmer); Charles & Josette Lenars (tc); Gianni Dagli Orti (br). **Getty Images**: Jon Arnold / AWL Images (clb); Science & Society Picture Library (bc); Michael Freeman / Taxi (bl). **SuperStock**: PhotoStock-Israel / age fotostock (tl). 66-67 **Corbis**: Ron Watts (background). 66 **Alamy Images**: The Art Archive (cr). **Dorling Kindersley**: Sakamoto Photo Research Laboratory (tr). **Dorling Kindersley**: Judith Miller / Wallis and Wallis (bl); The Science Museum, London (cb, c). **Getty Images**: Fotosearch Value (br). 67 **Alamy Images**: The Print Collector (tr). **Corbis**: Zhang Xiaoli / Epa (cra). **Getty Images**: DEA / G. Dagli Orti (br). 68-69 **Corbis**: Ron Watts (background). 68 **Alamy Images**: Peter Horree (c); INTERFOTO (tr). **Corbis**: Bettmann (cr). **Getty Images**: Hulton Archive / Hulton Royals Collection (bl); Werner Forman / Universal Images Group (cl); Gjon Mili / Time & Life Pictures (br). **SuperStock**: Fine Art Images (br). 69 **Alamy Images**: Prisma Archivo (t). **The Bridgeman Art Library**: Dinodia (cr); Araldo de Luca (c); Bettmann (cl). **Dorling Kindersley**: Rough Guides (tr/background). **Getty Images**: DEA / A. Jemolo (tl); Cute Kitten Images / Flickr (tr); Images Etc Ltd / Photographer's Choice RF (bc); Image Source (br). 70 **Getty Images**: Hoberman Collection / Universal Images Group (tc); Blake Kent / Design Pics (bl). 70-71 **Corbis**: Ron Watts (background). **Getty Images**: Dea Picture Library (bc). 71 **Getty Images**: Werner Forman / Universal Images Group (tr); Egyptian / The Bridgeman Art Library (cl)

Jacket images: Front: Angelo Hornak tc; **Dorling Kindersley**: Natural History Museum, London tl/ (Turquoise Ornament), Rough Guides bc, University Museum of Archaeology and Anthropology, Cambridge tl; *Back*: **Dorling Kindersley**: Egyptian Museum, Cairo bl

Wall chart: **Alamy Images**: The Art Archive cb/ (Qin Shihuangdi), Peter Horree br, Constantinos Iliopoulos cra; **Corbis**: Hoberman Collection fcr, cla/ (ZEUS COIN), Gianni Dagli Orti cla, bl; **Dorling Kindersley**: Ermine Street Guard crb; **Dreamstime.com**: Ralf Siemieniec cr; **Getty Images**: DEA / A. De Gregorio tl, DEA / A. Jemolo cl, J.D. Dallet / age fotostock cr, James L. Stanfield / National Geographic clb, Dea Picture Library / De Agostini Picture Library bc

All other images © Dorling Kindersley
For further information see:
www.dkimages.com